A FIEND IN *SHEEP'S* CLOTHING

THE TRAGIC PLIGHT *of the* AMERICAN CHRISTIAN

by

MICHAEL M. DILLARD

ISBN: 979-8-9989198-0-0

Library of Congress Control Number: 2025915550

First Edition

Published by Massive Endeavors Publishing
Ewa Beach, Hawaii

This book is a work of nonfiction. Unless otherwise noted, all references to people, events, and organizations are factual and accurately reflect the author's experience and research.

For information about bulk purchases, speaking engagements, or permissions, please contact:

Massive Endeavors Publishing
michael.dillard@massivekinetiks.com

Printed in the United States of America

Publishing Date: July 18, 2025

Dedications

To my Heavenly Father: Thank You Father for being my Dad! Thank You for sending Your Son Jesus to die for me that I might have life and have it more abundantly. Thank You for loving me. I love You Father!

To my Lord and Savior Jesus Christ: Thank You for taking my punishment on the cross. Thank you for faithfully walking with me through all the years I wandered in the valley of the shadow of death. Thank You for always showing me—beyond a shadow of a doubt—that You are real and that You love me. I love You Lord!

To my Master the Holy Spirit: Thank you for always being in the trenches with me. Thank you for keeping me and preserving me and my family from all evil. I love You Master!

To my lovely wife, Queen Angela the Beautiful: Thank you for your genuine love, kindness, and strength. You are the true Southern Belle that I prayed for and I'm so glad you're my wife! Always know that I am Yours and You are Mine. I love you Baby!

To my amazing Mom, Belinda Von B: Your faith, strength, humor, intellect, gift of gab, and resilience are woven into the very fabric of who I am. You taught me the value of hard work and the power of giving my very best effort. (No more automatic peanut crushers! Lol) Thank you so much for sending us to church when we were kids! Thank you for raising us (and not killing us). Lol. And by the way, sometimes you do have to be spooky about it! Lol. I love you Ma!

Acknowledgments

Writing a book of this nature is never the work of one person. It is the fruit of every conversation, prayer, and moment of encouragement shared by so many people who have walked beside me.

To my siblings, Derek and Ulanda—thank you for always having my back, even in those years when I was absent from our family. Thank you for always loving me and for reminding me of who I am and where I came from. I love you both so much!

To my brother from another mother, Wyatt— Thank you for being my Brother. You had my back during the lowest moments in my life and to this very day. I am grateful for your faithfulness, loyalty, and wisdom. I love you Bro!

To the pastors, mentors, and friends who have challenged me directly (and indirectly) by your words and actions to think deeply and to live faithfully with integrity. Thank you for helping to shape my convictions .

Finally, to every reader who picks up this book with an open heart—may you be inspired to love the Lord your God without compromise and to walk in the holiness that transforms individuals, marriages, families, cities, and nations.

Opening Prayer

Father,

Thank You for Your unfailing and jealous love for me. Please forgive me for all of the many ways that I have broken Your holy laws and commandments. Father, I pray that You would drive back and bind up any and every unclean spirit that would seek to hinder me from hearing and receiving these words from Your servant. Please grant me the faith to hear what Your Holy Spirit is saying to me. Please grant me the power to put it immediately into action in my life. I submit my body, soul, and spirit to You now and forevermore.

Thank You!

In Jesus' name,

Amen

Isaiah 1

Judah Called to Repentance

1 The vision of Isaiah the son of Amoz, which he saw concerning Judah and Jerusalem in the days of Uzziah, Jotham, Ahaz, *and* Hezekiah, kings of Judah.

The Wickedness of Judah

2 Hear, O heavens, and give ear, O earth!
For the Lord has spoken:
"I have nourished and brought up children,
And they have rebelled against Me;
3 The ox knows its owner
And the donkey its master's crib;
But Israel does not know,
My people do not consider."

4 Alas, sinful nation,
A people laden with iniquity,
A brood of evildoers,
Children who are corrupters!
They have forsaken the Lord,
They have provoked to anger
The Holy One of Israel,
They have turned away backward.

5 Why should you be stricken again?
You will revolt more and more.
The whole head is sick,

And the whole heart faints.
6 From the sole of the foot even to the head,
There is no soundness in it,
But wounds and bruises and putrefying sores;
They have not been closed or bound up,
Or soothed with ointment.

7 Your country *is* desolate,
Your cities *are* burned with fire;
Strangers devour your land in your presence;
And *it is* desolate, as overthrown by strangers.
8 So the daughter of Zion is left as a booth in a vineyard,
As a hut in a garden of cucumbers,
As a besieged city.
9 Unless the Lord of hosts
Had left to us a very small remnant,
We would have become like Sodom,
We would have been made like Gomorrah.

10 Hear the word of the Lord,
You rulers of Sodom;
Give ear to the law of our God,
You people of Gomorrah:
11 "To what purpose *is* the multitude of your sacrifices to Me?"
Says the Lord.
"I have had enough of burnt offerings of rams
And the fat of fed cattle.
I do not delight in the blood of bulls,
Or of lambs or goats.

12 "When you come to appear before Me,
Who has required this from your hand,
To trample My courts?
13 Bring no more futile sacrifices;
Incense is an abomination to Me.

The New Moons, the Sabbaths, and the calling of assemblies—
I cannot endure iniquity and the sacred meeting.
14 Your New Moons and your appointed feasts
My soul hates;
They are a trouble to Me,
I am weary of bearing *them*.
15 When you spread out your hands,
I will hide My eyes from you;
Even though you make many prayers,
I will not hear.
Your hands are full of blood.

16 "Wash yourselves, make yourselves clean;
Put away the evil of your doings from before My eyes.
Cease to do evil,
17 Learn to do good;
Seek justice,
Rebuke the oppressor;
Defend the fatherless,
Plead for the widow.

18 "Come now, and let us reason together,"
Says the Lord,
"Though your sins are like scarlet,
They shall be as white as snow;
Though they are red like crimson,
They shall be as wool.
19 If you are willing and obedient,
You shall eat the good of the land;
20 But if you refuse and rebel,
You shall be devoured by the sword";
For the mouth of the Lord has spoken.

The Degenerate City

21 How the faithful city has become a harlot!
It was full of justice;
Righteousness lodged in it,
But now murderers.
22 Your silver has become dross,
Your wine mixed with water.
23 Your princes *are* rebellious,
And companions of thieves;
Everyone loves bribes,
And follows after rewards.
They do not defend the fatherless,
Nor does the cause of the widow come before them.

24 Therefore the Lord says,
The Lord of hosts, the Mighty One of Israel,
"Ah, I will rid Myself of My adversaries,
And take vengeance on My enemies.
25 I will turn My hand against you,
And thoroughly purge away your dross,
And take away all your alloy.
26 I will restore your judges as at the first,
And your counselors as at the beginning.
Afterward you shall be called the city of righteousness, the faithful city."

27 Zion shall be redeemed with justice,
And her penitents with righteousness.
28 The destruction of transgressors and of sinners *shall be* together,
And those who forsake the Lord shall be consumed.
29 For they shall be ashamed of the terebinth trees
Which you have desired;
And you shall be embarrassed because of the gardens
Which you have chosen.

30 For you shall be as a terebinth whose leaf fades,
And as a garden that has no water.
31 The strong shall be as tinder,
And the work of it as a spark;
Both will burn together,
And no one shall quench *them*.

Author Keyword
Definitions & Biblical Parallels

Tragic – (*TRAH-jik*) - Pertaining to a grave, sorrowful condition arising from human failure, moral collapse, or divine abandonment—especially when the subject, once noble or spiritually favored, falls into deception, compromise, or ruin.

Biblical Parallel: Just as the prophet Isaiah lamented Israel's failure to walk in the ways of the Lord—despite all they had been given—the American Christian today mirrors that same tragedy. With unmatched religious freedom, abundant resources, and generational access to the gospel, many have chosen cultural conformity over covenant contriteness. The result is a spiritually impoverished people who believe they are rich in faith, yet walk in rebellion and self-deception.

"O that you had heeded My commandments!
Then your peace would have been like a river,
And your righteousness like the waves of the sea."
— Isaiah 48:18 (NKJV)

In this divine lament, God reveals not only His grief, but the greatness of what was forfeited. And so it is with the American Christian—a people with every opportunity to walk in power, purity, and purpose, yet tragically content with worldly pleasure over godly purpose.

Plight – (*PLYT* — rhymes with "flight") - A dire and entangled spiritual condition marked by confusion, self-deception, and estrangement from God—often appearing outwardly prosperous or pious but inwardly bankrupt and bound.

Biblical Parallel: This refers to the American Christian's condition of being trapped in cultural Christianity, lulled by comfort and avarice, unaware of their distance from true holiness and power.

Like the Laodicean church in Revelation 3:17 — "You say, 'I am rich; I have acquired wealth and do not need a thing.' But you do not realize that you are wretched, pitiful, poor, blind and naked."

Fiend – (*FEEND* — rhymes with "weaned") - A deceptive spiritual force or false representative of righteousness—one who, whether knowingly or unknowingly, operates under the guise of godliness but is, in truth, an agent of corruption, distortion, or destruction within the Church.

Biblical Parallel: Not merely an enemy from without, but a seducer from within—often appearing as a fellow believer, pastor, influencer, or movement that mimics the language of faith while undermining its substance. A fiend is the embodiment of counterfeit holiness—dressed in sheep's clothing, yet inwardly ravenous. Many American Christians are like the religious leaders confronted by John the Baptist, who appeared outwardly pious but were, in God's eyes, a brood of poisonous deceivers—symbols of judgment, not righteousness. Their presence corrupted others and provoked the wrath of God.

"But when he saw many of the Pharisees and Sadducees coming to his baptism, he said to them, 'Brood of vipers! Who warned you to flee from the wrath to come? Therefore bear fruits worthy of repentance…'"
— Matthew 3:7–8 (NKJV)

Table of Contents

Introduction

Pursue peace with all people, and holiness, without which no one will see the Lord: looking carefully lest anyone fall short of the grace of God; lest any root of bitterness springing up cause trouble, and by this many become defiled; lest there be any fornicator or profane person like Esau, who for one morsel of food sold his birthright. For you know that afterward, when he wanted to inherit the blessing, he was rejected, for he found no place for repentance, though he sought it diligently with tears. — **Hebrews 12:14–17 (NKJV)**

From its inception, the United States was conceived with an exceptional vision: one nation under God, indivisible, with liberty and justice for all. A new nation rooted in biblical moral law and liberty of conscience. Our Founding Fathers, whether devout or deist, broadly affirmed the moral weight of Holy Scripture. In the early American consciousness, Christian ethics were not merely private virtues but public necessities. Fast-forward to today, and a very different landscape has emerged.

Modern American Christianity stands at a precipice. Though cloaked in the language of faith, much of what passes for holy and acceptable Christian practices in the United States bears little resemblance to the fervent discipleship of the early Christian church or even the self-sacrificial evangelicalism of America's own spiritual awakenings. As a nation, we have gained unprecedented freedom — and yet somewhere along the line, somehow over the course of time, we have lost the very power of God that helped us to earn our freedom from the British monarchy. The American church has become, a toothless lion: religious in speech, consumeristic in spirit, and thus lacking the delivering power of the Holy Spirit to set the captives free and truly make a difference in our nation.

The reason for this is quite simple: we as a people and thus as a nation are lacking holiness. In Hebrews 12:14, we are instructed to pursue peace AND holiness. Many believers are focused on pursuing peace right now and understandably so. The stressors of life are at an all time high. A 2025 survey by Northwestern Mutual found that about 70% of Americans experience depression or anxiety over money, with 60% losing sleep due to financial worries. Among younger generations (Gen Z and millennials), burnout is occurring earlier—by age 25, many already face high levels of stress due to jobs (33%), finances (27%), and mental health (24%). Some attempt to find peace through spiritual disciplines like prayer. Others through holistic approaches like yoga and meditation. While pursuing peace is popular, pursuing holiness is not and that is definitely a BIG problem. Proverbs 14:34 tells us that righteousness exalts a nation.

Like a silent cancer, the lack of holiness is slowly killing our great nation from within. This book contends that American Christians are suffering from a tragic spiritual plight: a diluted American gospel, a distorted spiritual identity, and a dangerous complacency. Like Israel in the days of Jeremiah, we have exchanged living water for broken cisterns (Jer. 2:13). Many Christians living in America today have a form of godliness but deny its power (2 Tim. 3:5), living under spiritual bondage, idolatry and delusion without even knowing it. The great freedom we cherish in America has become our stumbling block. We are a people drunk on liberty, but starved of holiness. And without holiness NO ONE (*not even American Christians*) will see the Lord.

CHAPTER 1

The Idol of American Christianity

*"A nation cannot rise above the altar it neglects—nor can a church lead a
people back to the Most High God while bowing low to the gods of this culture."*
— Michael M. Dillard

Introductory Paragraph:

America's origin story is deeply interwoven with Scripture, moral law,
and a collective pursuit of liberty rooted in Judeo-Christian values.
While the Founding Fathers were not perfect men, they acknowledged a
divine moral authority, appealing to "the laws of nature and of nature's
God" in their declarations and decisions. But somewhere along the line,
reverence gave way to revision. Modern Christianity in America enjoys
unprecedented religious freedom—yet instead of leading culture, the
church has often become led by it. We must ask: how did a nation so
saturated with churches, resources, and religious broadcasting become so
spiritually bankrupt?

The Illusion of a Christian Majority in America

Statistically, over 60% of Americans still claim to be Christian. But
what does that truly mean today? It rarely reflects biblical discipleship
or the fruit of repentance. Many identify as Christian while embracing
ideologies and lifestyles that openly oppose the teachings of Christ. Much
like ancient Israel, modern believers can profess allegiance while living in
rebellion. This discrepancy exposes the illusion: the majority may claim
Christ, but few carry the cross.

The late revivalist Leonard Ravenhill once asked, "Are the things you are living for worth Christ dying for?" For many professing Christians in America, the answer is tragically "no." Their version of Christianity costs nothing, changes nothing, and demands nothing. It is a belief system of convenience, not conviction.

The Powerless Church: Like the Sons of Sceva

In Acts 19:13–16, the sons of Sceva attempted to cast out demons using the name of Jesus—yet had no relationship with Him. The demons responded, "Jesus I know, and Paul I know about, but who are you?" The result was public humiliation and physical defeat. This passage reveals the danger of form without power. Today's American Church often reflects this same impotence: great in number, loud in platform, yet unable to bring deliverance, healing, or transformation because the Spirit has been grieved or forsaken.

In a time when demonic activity is no longer hiding in the shadows, we need churches that walk in the power of the Spirit—not platforms driven by branding, marketing, or motivational slogans. But what we've seen instead is a slow and subtle exchange of fire for fog. The altar has been replaced by LED screens, the anointing by algorithms, and truth by trendiness.

Historical Reverence vs. Modern Revisionism

The founders of this nation may have had theological disagreements, but many shared one core belief: that liberty could not survive without morality, and morality could not stand without religion. George Washington, in his farewell address, warned:

"Of all the dispositions and habits which lead to political prosperity, religion and morality are indispensable supports."

John Adams echoed this when he wrote:

"Our Constitution was made only for a moral and religious people. It is wholly inadequate to the government of any other."

These were not passing religious platitudes. They were acknowledgments that freedom must be restrained by virtue—or it would collapse under the weight of its own indulgence. And yet, today, we see how virtue has been replaced by vanity, and truth by preference.

There's Only One Way to Make America Truly Great Again

True national restoration will never come through elections, policies, or programs—it begins at the altar. Righteousness exalts a nation, but sin is a reproach to any people. No movement can outvote rebellion against God. Until holiness returns to the pulpit and repentance returns to the pews, the decline will continue. The hope of this nation rests not in patriotism, but in personal and collective purity before the Lord.

This is not to say we should disengage from civil duty—but rather that civil duty without spiritual renewal is like rearranging furniture on a sinking ship. It may look orderly for a moment, but the outcome remains disaster unless the breach is sealed—and that breach is sin.

Denominational Drift and the Rise of Cultural Christianity

Many historic denominations, once guardians of orthodoxy, now openly bless sin under the guise of progress. From affirming lifestyles God clearly calls unholy, to ordaining leaders who reject the authority of Scripture, the slow apostasy of the American Church is no longer slow—it's celebrated. What once would have caused weeping now draws applause.

Today's cultural Christianity offers inspirational quotes without cross-bearing, blessing without brokenness, and favor without fear of God.

Churches compete for relevance, not reverence—creating consumer-driven experiences that feel more like theme parks than temples of the Most High God.

The Meaning of Reproach: A Transitive Warning

To reproach someone is to express disappointment or disapproval for conduct that is blameworthy or in need of change. It is a transitive verb—meaning action must be taken upon someone or something. God has every right to reproach His people, for we have traded the eternal for the entertaining, the sacred for the sensational, and the holy for the hollow.

The American Christian today stands as a living example of this reproach—a people meant to be salt and light, now dim and diluted. When the world cannot distinguish between the Church and itself, the Church has failed in its calling.

A Prophetic Reflection

There is a stirring in the spirit of many believers—an awareness that something is gravely wrong. They sense the Holy Spirit calling them out of religious showmanship and into sacred sobriety. It is a return to the narrow path, to the trembling at God's Word, to worship without manipulation or spectacle.

We don't need another influencer on a platform—we need intercessors at the altar. We don't need celebrity pastors—we need consecrated prophets.

We don't need smoke machines—we need the smoke of God's glory filling the temple again.

Transition Paragraph:

If the foundations be destroyed, what can the righteous do? They can repent, rebuild, and return. But to do so, the Church must first recognize its complicity in the decay. In the next chapter, we will examine how deception creeps in unnoticed, wearing sheep's clothing but carrying a wolf's appetite. These are not foreign enemies—they are fiends from within.

End of Chapter Review Questions:

1. How does the illusion of a "Christian majority" in America mask the true spiritual state of the Church?

    _____

    _____

2. In what ways does the story of the sons of Sceva parallel today's powerless church movements?

    _____

    _____

3. What does it mean to have form without power in modern Christianity?

    _____

    _____

4. What principles did America's early leaders tie to the preservation of freedom and morality?

    _____

    _____

5. How have denominations drifted from biblical orthodoxy in recent decades?

    _____

    _____

6. What are signs that a church or believer has embraced cultural comfort over covenant obedience?

    _____

    _____

7. How does the meaning of "reproach" help us better understand God's response to sin in the church?

_____

_____

8. What specific areas do you believe the modern church must repent of to see national restoration?

_____

_____

9. Why is righteousness essential for a nation to be truly great in God's eyes?

_____

_____

10. What role can you play in helping restore reverence, righteousness, and revival to the body of Christ?

_____

_____

CHAPTER 2

A Fiend in Sheep's Clothing

"Satan's most loyal foot soldiers often sit in church pews—convinced they're fighting for God while serving the purposes of hell." — **Michael M. Dillard**

Introduction

What if the greatest threat to the Church wasn't outside its walls, but seated quietly in its pews? What if the most destructive force at work in the house of God wasn't a flamboyant false prophet or a liberal political agenda—but the average, well-meaning, deceived churchgoer?

The "fiend in sheep's clothing" is rarely who we expect. We've been trained to scan the headlines for celebrity preachers, prosperity pimps, or the latest YouTube heretic. But the most common and effective agent of Satan's agenda doesn't need a spotlight. In fact, they often avoid it. They serve on committees, sing on praise teams, and volunteer with youth.

They speak in Christian clichés, post Bible verses on social media, and even tithe regularly. But they have never truly repented. Their hearts have not been transformed. And while they sincerely believe they're doing God's work, they are unwittingly advancing the enemy's cause.

Jesus warned us about such people:

> *"Many will say to Me on that day, 'Lord, Lord, have we not prophesied in Your name, cast out demons in Your name, and done many wonders in Your name?' And then I will declare to them, 'I never knew you; depart from Me, you who practice lawlessness!'"*
> **(Matthew 7:22–23, NKJV).**

The most tragic deception is the one that feels like salvation.

A Historical Overview of the Nicolaitans and Modern Church Parallels

Who Were the Nicolaitans?

In Revelation 2, Christ delivers messages to seven churches, and in two of them—Ephesus and Pergamum—He references a group He explicitly *hates*: the Nicolaitans.

> *"But this you have, that you hate the deeds of the Nicolaitans, which I also hate."* —**Revelation 2:6 (NKJV)**

> *"Thus you also have those who hold the doctrine of the Nicolaitans, which thing I hate."* —**Revelation 2:15 (NKJV)**

The Scriptures do not give an extended background on who these people were, but early church writings help fill in the gaps. The Nicolaitans were likely followers of Nicolas of Antioch, one of the seven men chosen to serve in Acts 6:5. According to Irenaeus, Hippolytus, and Clement of Alexandria, Nicolas later fell into heresy—teaching that Christians were free to indulge the flesh, engaging in sexual immorality and idolatrous feasts under the guise of spiritual liberty.

Clement of Alexandria wrote:

"They abandoned themselves to pleasure like goats, leading a life of self-indulgence. Their doctrine perverted grace into a license for immorality."

This early heresy was a perversion of the doctrine of grace—suggesting that since Christ had died for sins, believers were now free to sin without consequence. It combined lawlessness (antinomianism) with compromise, opening the door to pagan customs, temple orgies, and food sacrificed to idols—all while maintaining a superficial Christian identity.

Modern Nicolaitanism in the American Church

Though ancient in origin, the spirit of Nicolaitanism has never left. It has merely changed form. Today, it takes the shape of cultural Christianity—a watered-down gospel that permits sin under the banner of grace, replaces conviction with convenience, and trades holiness for entertainment.

The core tenets remain the same:

1. Grace without repentance
2. Faith without obedience
3. Belonging without transformation

This false doctrine manifests in phrases like:

- "God knows my heart."
- "Nobody's perfect."
- "Jesus hung out with sinners, so why can't we?"
- "Love is love."

These slogans bypass the call to righteousness and make sin seem normal—even virtuous. They offer a form of godliness while denying its power (2 Tim. 3:5).

Today's Nicolaitan spirit is found in churches that:

- Celebrate sin in the name of inclusivty
- Use secular music to "attract the lost"
- Prioritize performance over presence
- Avoid preaching on sin, judgment, or hell
- Invite celebrities but ignore consecration

This spiritual compromise is everywhere—from liberal denominations to evangelical megachurches. Its seductive pull is emotional, affirming, non-confrontational. It tells people what they *want* to hear, not what they *need* to hear.

"The Church today is more interested in being accepted by the world than being approved by God." —**Leonard Ravenhill,**
Why Revival Tarries

False Conversions: A Doctrinal Crisis

At the heart of Nicolaitanism is a false conversion epidemic. Many in our churches have never actually been born again. They have walked aisles, repeated prayers, and joined ministries—but they have never repented. They have responded to an emotional appeal or a motivational sermon but not to the gospel of the cross.

David Wilkerson observed:

"Our churches are filled with people who've made decisions but have never made disciples."

Jesus made it clear in the parable of the sower (Luke 8:4–15) that not every seed takes root. Some fall on rocky ground—received with joy, but without depth. Others are choked by the cares of life and the deceitfulness of riches. Only the seed that falls on good ground, dies, and then produces fruit, represents true salvation.

The Appeal of Deception

Why are so many drawn to this false gospel? Because it's easy. The true gospel says:

- Die to yourself.
- Repent of sin.
- Follow Christ no matter the cost.

The false gospel says:

- Be yourself.
- Embrace your truth.
- God is love—He wouldn't send you to hell.

"People don't reject the Bible because it contradicts itself. They reject it because it contradicts them." —**Voddie Baucham**

It feeds the ego while starving the soul. It's psychologically soothing—but eternally damning.

Comparison Table & Exposition

Parallels Between the Nicolaitans and the American Church

The spirit of Nicolaitanism thrives today not because it's overtly demonic, but because it disguises itself as *familiar, harmless Christianity*. It blends truth with error, godliness with carnality, and grace with rebellion. It is spiritual syncretism—a fusion of heaven's vocabulary with hell's priorities.

This perverse mixture is why Jesus didn't just "disapprove" of the Nicolaitans—He hated their deeds and doctrines. It is divine language rarely used, signaling extreme corruption among those who claimed to follow Him.

Below is a comparison table outlining the parallels between Nicolaitan practices and common American Christian behaviors:

Comparison Table: Nicolaitan Practices vs. American Christian Parallels

Nicolaitan Practices	American Christian Parallels
Taught liberty as license to sin	"God's grace covers everything—I don't need to change."
Blended with pagan culture and idolatry	Adoption of secular trends: zodiac signs, manifestation, "Christian yoga," etc.
Justified sexual immorality	Normalization of cohabitation, LGBTQ+ affirmation in pulpits and pews

Nicolaitan Practices	American Christian Parallels
Ate food sacrificed to idols	Spiritual compromise for career, comfort, or political gain
Claimed Christian identity while living in sin	Professing faith but denying Christ's lordship over lifestyle
Rejected apostolic authority and correction	Disregard for pastoral rebuke or biblical church discipline
Appealed to emotions, not truth	Worship based on feelings, not theology; sermons as motivational TED Talks
Used God's name for personal advancement	Prosperity gospel and platform obsession

Exposition: A Doctrine of Demonic Mixture

The Nicolaitans did not outwardly renounce Jesus. That would have been too obvious. Instead, they presented a counterfeit Christianity—one where *Jesus was Savior but not Lord,* where *grace excused sin instead of transforming sinners,* and where *discipleship was optional.*

This is the **exact condition** Paul warned of when he wrote:

> *"For the time will come when they will not endure sound doctrine, but according to their own desires, because they have itching ears, they will heap up for themselves teachers; and they will turn their ears away from the truth, and be turned aside to fables."* **—2 Timothy 4:3–4 (NKJV)**

That time isn't coming—it's here. We have created entire church cultures built around entertainment, emotionalism, and affirmation—while quietly crucifying repentance, holiness, and truth.

"The modern church has decided that it's better to offend God than to offend man." —**David Wilkerson**

And what's worse, many believe they are walking in truth. Like the Pharisees, they evangelize, serve, and even cast out demons—but without true repentance, they are strangers to Christ. These are not enemies from the outside—they are **fiends in sheep's clothing**, embedded in the very heart of the church.

"There are many in our churches who are not backslidden—they've never front-slid." —**Leonard Ravenhill**

Real Church Examples & Voices of Warning

The Tragic Allure of Compromised Megachurches

Across America, many of the nation's largest churches have adopted a **seeker-sensitive** model that mirrors the Nicolaitan spirit. While not every megachurch falls into this trap, a disturbing number have exchanged biblical conviction for cultural affirmation.

These ministries boast sprawling campuses, multimillion-dollar budgets, and millions of followers on social media. But what is often absent from their pulpits is any mention of:

- The blood of Jesus
- The cross and crucified life
- The judgment to come
- The demand for repentance and holiness

Instead, sermons focus on self-esteem, goal-setting, and breakthrough— as if Jesus came to improve your vibe, not to destroy the works of the devil (1 John 3:8). Sin is rarely named. Hell is almost never mentioned. And instead of being called out of Babylon, believers are taught to build better lives within it.

"In many churches today, the Holy Spirit could leave and no one would notice. The show would go on, the lights would still flash, the fog machines would still blow, and the people would still clap."
—David Wilkerson, The Vision

Many such churches defend this approach by citing attendance growth or social media metrics. But size is not the measure of success in God's economy—faithfulness is.

"God does not bless a church because it's big. He blesses a church because it's obedient." **—Charles Stanley**

Celebrity Culture in the Sanctuary

Another sign of compromise is the rise of the celebrity Christian—preachers who are more influencer than intercessor. In some cases, they:

- Avoid offending the culture to protect their brand
- Invite secular entertainers to church platforms
- Appear on magazine covers while never being seen in the prayer room

This obsession with image over intimacy has created a generation that equates style with substance. Worship has become a concert. Preaching has become performance. And the presence of God has been replaced by production value.

As John MacArthur boldly warned:

"When church becomes entertainment, and the pulpit becomes a platform for opinion rather than exposition, we are no longer shepherds—we are performers. And the sheep are starving."

Faithful Churches: The Remnant Still Stands

But not all have bowed to compromise.

Across the nation, there remains a remnant of churches—small and large—who refuse to conform. These churches:

- Preach the full gospel, including sin, repentance, and hell
- Call believers to holy living and prayer
- Refuse to dilute the message to appeal to the culture
- Value presence over performance, truth over trends

These are churches that may not go viral, but they go deep. They are not known by crowds, but by the *cloud*—God's presence in their midst.

They are the ones who still cry out like Isaiah: *"Here am I. Send me."*
They still weep over sin.
They still believe in deliverance.
They still tarry at the altar.
They still walk in fear of the Lord.

> *"We don't need another method. We need another Pentecost."*
> **—Leonard Ravenhill**

These remnant churches are not perfect—but they are postured. They are not applauded by the world—but they are approved by heaven.

> *"If God removed His hand from America today, most churches wouldn't even know it for weeks."* **—David Wilkerson**

Revival or Reprobation

We stand at a crossroad. The American Church can either continue in the way of the Nicolaitans—pursuing relevance at the cost of righteousness—or return to the old paths of biblical truth, repentance, and Spirit-filled power.

"The church used to be a lightning bolt—now it's a cruise ship."
—Leonard Ravenhill

The tragedy? Many think they're walking with God when they're not.

Unless we awaken to this deception and confront it boldly within our own congregations, we may find ourselves busy doing church—but devoid of Christ.

"The most terrifying words in Scripture are not about hellfire. They are, 'I never knew you.'"—**John MacArthur**

The Rich Young Ruler: When the Word Confronts the Heart

The gospel is not a suggestion; it is a summons. And the response reveals everything.

In Luke 18:18–25, a rich young ruler approached Jesus—eager, curious, respectful. He had kept the commandments, performed the rituals, and was likely admired as a moral man. But when confronted with the actual words of God in the flesh, he balked.

Jesus said to him, *"One thing you still lack. Sell all that you have and distribute to the poor, and you will have treasure in heaven; and come, follow Me."*

But the man went away sorrowful.

Why?

Because the call of Christ exposed his idol. Though he had religion, he lacked surrender. He wanted heaven, but not if it cost him his comforts. He wanted righteousness, but not if it meant relinquishing control. He wanted Jesus as Savior—but not as Lord.

This, too, is the tragic plight of the modern American Christian.

We want the benefits of righteousness without the burden of obedience. We want deliverance, but not discipline. We want worship without sacrifice. We want transformation without crucifixion. Like the rich young ruler, we walk away grieved—not because Christ is unjust, but because we love our own version of the faith more than His.

The Heart of the Matter

A fiend in sheep's clothing isn't just the celebrity preacher preaching false doctrine. It's the average believer who sings about surrender but clutches their sin. It's the pew-sitter who claps at truth but lives in compromise. It's the lay leader who loves ministry but neglects holiness.

This is what makes this chapter so piercing—because it doesn't merely point outward. It draws a circle around **us**. It challenges the reader to ask: *Am I truly surrendered to Jesus Christ, or have I adopted a cultural Christianity that looks godly but lacks the cross?*

The Nicolaitans weren't outsiders. They were **churchgoers**.

So, too, today—our greatest threat isn't necessarily the world around us, but the unrepented world **within us**. It's the lukewarm heart. The hidden rebellion. The compromised witness.

The false assurance that we can belong to Christ while still belonging to Babylon.

We cannot.

A Fiend in Sheep's Clothing—Defined by Fruit

Jesus said, *"You will know them by their fruits."* (Matthew 7:16)

Not their words.
Not their theology.
Not their social following.

But by their fruit.

A fiend in sheep's clothing may appear loyal, generous, eloquent, and even powerful. But when examined, their fruit is rotten. There is no power over sin. No joy in obedience. No true hunger for righteousness. No transformation that reflects the character of Christ.

And this must bring us to a decision.

Will we continue to be part of the camouflage—pretending everything is well while sin festers beneath the surface? Or will we tear the wool from our own eyes and return to the one true Shepherd?

Transition Paragraph:

Before we can walk in the light, we must first recognize the darkness we've tolerated. The deception of Nicolaitan compromise is not just theological—it is deeply personal, and painfully present. But exposure is mercy. As we peel back the layers of counterfeit faith, we now turn our attention to the subtle poison of **syncretism**—a blending of the sacred and profane. In the next chapter, we'll examine how broken altars and blended threads have created a confused church, powerless to resist the culture it was meant to transform.

End of Chapter Review Questions

1. In what ways might Nicolaitan compromise be subtly present in your own life or church community?

   _____

   _____

2. Have you ever been drawn to a version of the gospel that promised freedom without repentance? What was the result?

   _____

   _____

3. How does the story of the rich young ruler challenge the way you view surrender and obedience?

_____

_____

4. Are there areas in your life where you acknowledge Christ as Savior but not as Lord? What needs to change?

_____

_____

5. How can you discern between a genuine move of God and one that merely imitates His presence?

_____

_____

6. Have you ever seen emotionalism or performance take the place of truth and transformation in a church setting?

_____

_____

7. What does it mean to you to "come out from among them and be separate"? Are you willing to be set apart—even if it costs you relationships or comfort?

_____

_____

8. How can you cultivate discernment so you're not deceived by spiritual-sounding language or movements?

_____

_____

9. What practical steps can you take this week to re-align your life with the true gospel of Jesus Christ?

_____

_____

10. Do you know someone who might be caught in a form of cultural Christianity? How can you lovingly share truth with them?

_____

_____

CHAPTER 3

Blended Threads and Broken Altars

"God never asked us to blend in—He called us to burn brightly. But when the holy is stitched to the profane, the altar collapses under the weight of our compromise." — **Michael M. Dillard**

Introduction

The Church was never meant to be a chameleon. From the moment God called Israel out of Egypt, His instruction was clear: "You shall be holy to Me, for I the Lord am holy and have separated you from the peoples, that you should be Mine" (Leviticus 20:26, ESV).

The Lord gave Israel strict commands not to blend what He had separated. In Leviticus 19:19, God tells His people not to wear garments made of mixed fabrics. In today's church, the threads have been blended.

Cultural Christianity has woven together the commandments of God with the ideologies of the world. The result is a garment that may appear spiritual but lacks power and purity.

"And when My angel goes before you and brings you to the Amorites, Hittites, Perizzites, Canaanites, Hivites, and Jebusites, and I blot them out, you shall not bow down to their gods nor serve them, nor do as they do, but you shall utterly overthrow them and break their pillars in pieces." — **Exodus 23:23–24 (ESV)**

While seemingly trivial, this command symbolized something deeper: God's insistence on purity and separation. Just as two dissimilar fibers were not to be woven together, God's people were not to mix His holy standards with pagan culture. This verse reveals that God never intended for His people to adopt the practices of the nations around them. He commands complete separation—no bowing, no serving, no mimicking.

Yet the American Church has not only forgotten her distinction—she has surrendered it. Somewhere between cultural accommodation and desperate relevance, we began stitching foreign threads into the fabric of our worship. We wove the priorities of empire into the pattern of the Kingdom. We mixed worldly customs with sacred commands. And what emerged was not a radiant Bride—but a confused and powerless people kneeling at broken altars built with borrowed blueprints. In the chart below we can see the parallels between Canaanite practices and those of today's church.

Modern Parallels to Canaanite Practice

Canaanite/Baal/Ashtoreth Practices	Modern-Day Church Equivalents
Temple prostitution	Sexual immorality among leadership
Child sacrifice (Molech worship)	Abortion normalization and silence
Idolatrous feasts and orgies	"Christian" conferences with worldly excess
Sorcery and divination	Christianized astrology and manifesting
Blended worship with idols	Mixing secular songs into worship sets

Syncretism is the fusion of competing ideologies under the banner of peace. It is the altar of mixture—a spiritual compromise that invites God's name while violating His nature. And it is nothing new.

From the golden calf at Sinai to the high places in ancient Judah, God's people have always been tempted to blend the sacred with the secular. But each time, the result was the same: judgment, confusion, and spiritual paralysis.

In today's America, we see the same thing. Churches that claim the name of Christ while hosting drag queen story hours. Congregations that preach inclusion but reject repentance. Ministries that invoke the Spirit but deny His sanctifying power.

This chapter is a call to tear the unclean thread from the garment and to rebuild the altar on the foundation of holiness. Because unless we confront the mixture in our worship, we will never walk in the fullness of His power.

The Coexist Movement and Modern-Day Mixture

On bumpers, billboards, and social feeds, one word has been elevated as the ultimate virtue: coexist. The idol of coexistence—celebrating every religion and lifestyle in the name of tolerance—has become popular even among Christians. It's marketed as tolerance. Celebrated as unity. Worn like a badge of honor.

But beneath the surface, this popular ideology carries a far more dangerous spiritual implication—it seeks to flatten all faiths into one.

The "Coexist" logo—featuring religious symbols from Islam, Judaism, Christianity, Wicca, Taoism, and more—represents not just peaceful tolerance, but the theological blending of incompatible worldviews. And while the original intent may have been cultural harmony, the spiritual effect is devastating when adopted by the Church. The "Coexist" bumper sticker may seem inclusive, but it ultimately encourages compromise, not conviction.

By embracing "coexistence" in the wrong context, many Christians have unknowingly diluted the gospel. The message of Jesus as "the way, the truth, and the life" (John 14:6) has been softened to "a way among many." The exclusive claims of Christ have been exchanged for an inclusive message that offends no one—especially not the gods of this age.

25

Syncretism doesn't start with open rebellion. It begins with harmless partnerships, watered-down sermons, and a desire to avoid conflict. It feels noble. It sounds compassionate. But its fruit is compromise, not conversion. Likewise, movements such as the "gay Christian church," the "gospel of inclusion" championed by the late Carlton Pearson, and institutions like the Unitarian Universalist church have distorted the gospel. These teachings embrace lifestyles clearly condemned by Scripture and often deny foundational truths, such as the existence of hell. Paul warned about such deceptions, calling them man-made doctrines of demons (1 Timothy 4:1).

The problem isn't that Christians live among people of other faiths. The problem arises when believers begin adopting their practices, justifying their philosophies, or redefining Scripture to be more "welcoming."

It's not just an issue in theology. It's become embedded in:

- Worship music that references the divine in vague, ambiguous terms, so it can be sung in interfaith gatherings.

- Pulpit language that never names sin or repentance but celebrates "spiritual journeys."

- Partnerships with organizations that reject Christ but align with "social good," giving the appearance of shared mission.

God does not ask His people to hate others. He commands us to love—but never at the expense of truth. Jesus dined with sinners, but He never compromised with sin. He touched lepers, but never legitimized the disease.

And yet in our modern attempts to be "relevant," many churches now affirm what God condemns, confuse kindness with agreement, and mistake silence for wisdom.

Syncretism has rebranded itself as progress. But in heaven's eyes, it is still idolatry—no less offensive now than it was at Sinai.

The altar of God was always meant to be holy, separate, and untouched by the tools of man (Exodus 20:25). Yet in today's Church, the altar has been cluttered with foreign stones, erected on the approval of man rather than the presence of God.

And when the altar is compromised, so is the fire.

Witchcraft in the Modern Church: Adultery with Babylon the Harlot

One of the ways the altar is compromised is through a spirit of witchcraft. This is one of the reasons the American church has become so weak. The spirit of witchcraft has been allowed into pulpits across the nation insidiously covered up so it doesn't "look like" witchcraft.

It hides itself in a variety of seemingly normal, harmless and commonplace activities loved by Christians the world over. Let's see what the Bible says about witchcraft:

> *"For rebellion is as the sin of witchcraft, and stubbornness is as iniquity and idolatry."* - **1 Samuel 15:23 (NKJV)**

Rebellion, spiritual compromise, and stubbornness are no small matters in the sight of the Lord. They are on par with witchcraft—and sadly, witchcraft has found new expression within the church.

Yoga, smudging, energy healing, Christian tarot, "intergenerational healing" ceremonies—these are not innocent trends. They are doctrines of demons, clothed in language that appears harmless.

Yoga's Spiritual Roots

Millions of Americans—including a significant percentage of Christians—participate in yoga. But its origins are far from neutral. Yoga emerged from Vedic and Hindu spirituality as a method to awaken the kundalini spirit and achieve unity with Hindu gods. Even the poses themselves are acts of worship to these deities.

"Do not turn to mediums or seek out spiritists..." — **Leviticus 19:31**

"...Some will abandon the faith and follow deceiving spirits and things taught by demons." — **1 Timothy 4:1**

"Come out of her, My people..." — **Revelation 18:4**

In short, the LORD hates witchcraft. If we truly love Him, we must hate the things He hates. We must not idolize it or celebrate it in any form— *this is a serious offense before a holy God!*

The Repentant Town in Acts

"Many of those who had practiced magic brought their books together and burned them in the sight of all." — **Acts 19:18–19**

In response to revival, the people of Ephesus didn't host a forum about coexistence—they destroyed every trace of witchcraft. May the modern church have the same boldness.

Halloween and the Spirit of Compromise

Halloween is one of the holiest days for Satanists and witches. Rebranding it as Trunk or Treat—with costumes and candy—does not sanctify its origins. The same goes for Harry Potter books, Pokémon, or ghost-hunting reality shows—they all fascinate people with the forbidden.

"I'm glad Christian parents let their children worship the devil at least one night out of the year. Welcome to Halloween."
— **Anton LaVey, founder of the Church of Satan**

Consequences of Allowing Witchcraft into the Pulpit

Witch covens strategically send agents (witches) into churches to quench the Spirit, stifle worship, and destroy fellowships. This is a known practice used to take spiritual dominion over the region the church is operating in. When this tactic is employed, the primary target is to eliminate the worship, for it is God's invitation to dwell among His people and the demons will not be able to operate freely with God's presence filling the sanctuary.

Psalm 22:3 states, *"But you are holy, enthroned on the praises of Israel."*

When a spirit of witchcraft is welcomed into the pulpit, knowingly or not:

- The presence of God withdraws.

- Praise becomes lifeless. To be clear this doesn't necessarily mean that the music won't sound upbeat and stir the emotions. Rather the presence of God is not drawn to this sort of music and so there is literally no life in it.

- Sermons lack the fire of the anointing. Without God's anointing on a pastor or preacher, the sermons are just fine sounding orations. The anointing of God is what sets ablaze the words of a pastor or preacher; it's what drives back the evil spirits and sets the stage for spiritual breakthrough and deliverance.

- Altars consistently remain empty during the invitation to prayer after the sermon.

- Not very many conversions will take place on Sundays.

- Not many new people being drawn to the church. Why is this? Because when pastors invite Jezebel into the pulpit with them, either knowingly or unknowingly, the tainted messages which are being preached are no longer lifting up Jesus. And thus the people will not be drawn to Him in that place. Ultimately the health and longevity of the church will suffer. As members leave the church for various reasons (age, health, job, family responsibilities, etc.) and do not get replaced with new members tithes will continue to drop, ministries will either become ineffective or non-existent as they lack the people to fulfill the duties. Which in turn drives people to find other churches that can provide the ministries that they need in their life.

- Division creeps in. Internal fights, drama and accusations flare up to eventually become the norm amongst staff members and those overseeing various ministries.

The church will continue to suffer until the spirit of witchcraft is removed. In short, Jezebel must be forcibly removed from the pulpit, as she will not go willingly.

> *"You cannot serve Jesus while clinging to Jezebel. You cannot bow before the cross of Christ while keeping a foot in the circle of Satan. God is not mocked."* **- Michael M. Dillard**

Tolerating That Woman Jezebel

Revelation 2:20 says, *"You tolerate that woman Jezebel, who calls herself a prophetess..."*

God's people must not allow Jezebel into their personal lives. Especially those who oversee God's flock.

You cannot tolerate that woman Jezebel in your personal life behind closed doors and then think that God's Spirit will be with you in the pulpit.

He will not because you have unwittingly joined yourself with that unholy spirit and where you go, it (the spirit of witchcraft) goes. Even in the pulpit.

This reminds me of the account of Samson. After Delilah cut his hair, Samson didn't realize that the Spirit of God wasn't with him; he didn't realize that his great strength was gone.

When Delilah saw that he had told her all his heart, she sent and called for the lords of the Philistines, saying, "Come up once more, for he has told me all his heart." So the lords of the Philistines came up to her and brought the money in their hand. Then she lulled him to sleep on her knees, and called for a man and had him shave off the seven locks of his head. Then she began to torment him, and his strength left him. And she said,

"The Philistines are upon you, Samson!" So he awoke from his sleep, and said, "I will go out as before, at other times, and shake myself free!" But he did not know that the Lord had departed from him. Then the Philistines took him and put out his eyes, and brought him down to Gaza. They bound him with bronze fetters, and he became a grinder in the prison.

Judges 16:18-21 NKJV

Can you see the real issue that ultimately cost Samson his two eyes and his very life? Most people will tell you it was the fact that he violated the Nazirite vow by allowing his hair to be cut. That's too surface though. If you peel back the layers, you'll see that his heart belonged to Delilah (the woman with a Jezebel spirit) and not the Lord. He never divulged the secret of his great strength to anyone else but her. He loved her. He loved her more than he loved the Lord. His tolerance with that Jezebel spirit cost him his anointing.

His supernatural empowering was gone and he could no longer do the thing the Lord had created him to do...until he repented.

And so it is with all who tolerate that spirit in their lives. It will cost them their anointing.

They may still stand in the pulpit and deliver a message but there won't be any real power in it because the Lord won't be there. Let's see how this plays out in Ezekiel 8:6-12:

Furthermore He said to me, "Son of man, do you see what they are doing, the great abominations that the house of Israel commits here, to make Me go far away from My sanctuary? Now turn again, you will see greater abominations." So He brought me to the door of the court; and when I looked, there was a hole in the wall. Then He said to me, "Son of man, dig into the wall"; and when I dug into the wall, there was a door. And He said to me, "Go in, and see the wicked abominations which they are doing there." So I went in and saw, and there—every sort of creeping thing, abominable beasts, and all the idols of the house of Israel, portrayed all around on the walls. And there stood before them seventy men of the elders of the house of Israel… each man had a censer in his hand, and a thick cloud of incense went up. Then He said to me, "Son of man, have you seen what the elders of the house of Israel do in the dark, every man in the room of his idols? For they say, 'The Lord does not see us, the Lord has forsaken the land.'"

Please. If any of your personal activities have anything to do with witchcraft, and I mean anything at all, you must go before the Lord and repent. Right now. You must repent for loving that Jezebel spirit, for protecting it, defending it, and giving your heart to it. You must immediately get rid of (i.e., throw out, destroy, or even burn like the people of Ephesus in Acts 19:18–19) any and all things having to do with any form of witchcraft: fantasy books, games, movies, toys/figurines, et cetera. Also get rid of anything relating to dragons and dragon lore.

There's only one being in the entire Bible referred to as a dragon and that's Satan, which by the way is also an anagram for... you guessed it: Santa

"So the great dragon was cast out, that serpent of old, called the Devil and Satan, who deceives the whole world; he was cast to the earth, and his angels were cast out with him." - **Revelation 12:9 (NKJV)**

"He laid hold of the dragon, that serpent of old, who is the Devil and Satan, and bound him for a thousand years."
- Revelation 20:2 (NKJV)

On a personal note, the Lord convicted me and Angela about watching certain tv shows and movie franchises. See below:

Game of Thrones / House of Dragons - Full of dragons. 'Nuff said.

Star Wars - Full of witchcraft. Always has been. Always will be. See below.

How "The Force" Ties into Witchcraft

1. The term "The Force" — popularized by the Star Wars franchise — is portrayed as a mystical energy field that binds all living things and gives Jedi (and Sith) their supernatural power. But outside of fiction, "The Force" is a real concept in occult and witchcraft practices.

2. In witchcraft and New Age circles, "the force" is often used to describe a neutral energy that can be manipulated by spells, intentions, and rituals. It's frequently referred to as:

    • "Life force"

    • "Universal energy"

    • "Chi" (in Eastern religions)

    • "Mana," "Prana," or simply "The Power"

Witches and occultists are taught that this force can be harnessed— either for "white" (benevolent) or "black" (malicious) magic. This is a trick of the devil to get many to believe that there are good forms of magic/witchcraft. However, regardless of whether the magic is white or black magic, it is all evil in the sight of the Lord. The very notion of good or benevolent magic is an oxymoron.

Examples from Witchcraft Resources

In Wicca and other pagan practices:

Spells often begin by "calling upon the force of nature" or "channeling the universal energy."

Some covens openly describe spellwork as "manipulating the force."

In ceremonial magic, practitioners invoke "forces of the elements" (earth, air, fire, water, spirit) to fuel their rituals.

So, "the Force" is a very known term among witches—used as a description of real spiritual energies that they believe they can command and control.

Why This Matters for Christians

Scripture never describes God's power as an impersonal force we can access at will. Instead:

- Power belongs to God alone (Psalm 62:11).

- The Holy Spirit operates according to God's will, not ours (1 Corinthians 12:11).

- Attempting to manipulate unseen powers outside of God's Word is strictly forbidden (Deuteronomy 18:10–12).

What looks like harmless fantasy—whether it's "The Force" in pop culture, energy manipulation in yoga, reiki, the world of wizarding and spellcraft in Harry Potter, manga or summoning magical creatures in Pokémon—can subtly desensitize believers to the very real spiritual dangers connected to witchcraft.

How to Deal with Jezebel

We must not tolerate Jezebel in our lives in any shape, form, or fashion. There is only one way to effectively deal with Jezebel and that is: You must put her to death like King Jehu.

Now when Jehu had come to Jezreel, Jezebel heard of it; and she put paint on her eyes and adorned her head, and looked through a window. Then, as Jehu entered at the gate, she said, "Is it peace, Zimri, murderer of your master?" And he looked up at the window and said, "Who is on my side? Who?" So two or three eunuchs looked out at him. Then he said, "Throw her down." So they threw her down, and some of her blood spattered on the wall and on the horses; and he trampled her underfoot. -- 2 Kings 9:30-33 NKJV

Did you see how Jehu dealt with Jezebel?? He didn't entertain any conversation with her or engage with her at all. He merely gave the command to throw her down to her death.

God decreed Jezebel's death as divine judgment because of her deep involvement in witchcraft, idolatry, sexual immorality, and the persecution of God's prophets. She embodied everything God detested in leadership—manipulation, spiritual corruption, and the promotion of Baal worship over devotion to Yahweh. Jezebel used her royal influence to institutionalize Baal worship and erect altars and Asherah poles, replacing the worship of Yahweh with demonic paganism. We see mention of her witchcraft in a conversation between King Jehu and Jezebel's son Joram in 2 Kings 9:22.

"When Joram saw Jehu he said, 'Is it peace, Jehu?' So he answered, 'What peace, as long as the harlotries of your mother Jezebel and her witchcraft are so many?'"

Again, there is no form of witchcraft that is harmless or benevolent. All witchcraft is sin in the eyes of the Lord. Cease and desist all activities that deal with witchcraft in your personal lives. Repent and reclaim your anointing.

Rebuilding the Altars—What True Worship Requires

Every revival in Scripture begins with a confrontation. Not a tent meeting. Not a music festival. Not a new podcast series.

A confrontation—between God's holiness and the people's compromise.

Before Elijah could call down fire on Mount Carmel, he had to first repair the altar of the Lord that had been torn down (1 Kings 18:30). Before Nehemiah could restore Jerusalem's walls, the people had to return to the reading of the Law.

Before Josiah's reforms, the Book of the Law had to be rediscovered in the temple. There is no glory without consecration, and there is no fire without a righteous altar.

But what does it mean to rebuild the altar today?

It means we must first tear down what doesn't belong.

The American Church has built altars that glorify men, amplify emotion, and showcase performance—but do not honor God. Altars of smoke and light. Altars of popularity and politics. Altars of self-help messages disguised as sermons. These altars may draw crowds, but they do not draw heaven.

To rebuild the true altar is to return to:

- The Word of God as the final authority. Not culture, not trends, not feelings—but Scripture alone.

- Prayer as the fuel, not the afterthought. In Acts 2, power came after they waited in one accord, not after a well-curated schedule.

- Holiness as the standard, not legalism but surrender. God's grace empowers righteousness, not excuses rebellion.

- Repentance as the doorway, not just belief. A changed mind and a changed life are the proof of a redeemed heart.

- Worship that invites presence over performance. True worship may sound beautiful—but more importantly, it breaks chains. This actually happens first in your prayer closet. If you're not doing it behind closed doors, do not expect to go to church and enter the presence of the Lord during that brief worship session.

- We must stop trying to build altars that attract people and start building altars that attract God.

The Cost of Mixture

The priests in Malachi's day offered blind, crippled, and diseased animals on the altar—and dared to call it worship (Malachi 1:6–10). God's response was clear: *"Oh that one of you would shut the temple doors!"*

Why?

Because offering polluted worship is worse than offering none at all.

When we mix what is holy with what is profane, we invite judgment instead of presence. We sow confusion instead of conviction. We raise up a generation that doesn't know what is acceptable to the Lord—and as a result, we raise up churches with no fear of God, no deliverance, and no spiritual authority.

To rebuild the altar, we must call sin what God calls it. We must tear down our idols of comfort, compromise, and cultural relevance. And we must return to the simplicity and power of the cross.

The blood still speaks.

The fire still falls.

But not on strange altars.

Lessons from Abraham's Altars and Today's Call to Consecration

The Bible introduces Abraham not just as the father of faith—but as a man of altars. Wherever Abraham went, he didn't simply build wealth or influence; he built places of worship. His altars were not decorative—they were declarative: "God brought me here, and I belong to Him."

From Shechem to Bethel, from Hebron to Moriah, Abraham marked his journey with devotion. And each altar tells us something about the kind of worship God still honors.

1. The Altar of Obedience (Genesis 12:7)

When Abraham arrived in the land God promised, his first act wasn't to scout the terrain or negotiate with locals—it was to build. He didn't wait for favorable circumstances. He responded in faith. The altar was his first priority, not his last resort.

Too often today, obedience is delayed until God proves Himself. We wait for signs, comfort, and guarantees. But Abraham shows us that true worship begins with surrender—even when the future is uncertain.

2. The Altar of Return (Genesis 13:4)

After a detour into Egypt driven by fear, Abraham returned to Bethel—to the very altar he had built before. This wasn't just about location—it was about repentance.

How many of us need to return to the place where we once communed with God? To restore the fire that once burned on the altar of our hearts?

The American Church is long overdue for a return—to the Word, to holiness, to fervent prayer.

God is not waiting for a new strategy. He is calling His people to return to what was abandoned.

3. The Altar of Covenant (Genesis 15:9–10)

In Genesis 15, God instructs Abraham to prepare a covenant sacrifice—cutting animals in two as a sign of irrevocable agreement. This was no casual ritual. It was bloody, sacred, and binding.

The Church today has forgotten the covenantal cost of grace. We speak of blessings, not burdens. Of rights, but not responsibilities. But true covenant requires blood. It demands loyalty. And it invites fire from heaven only when the sacrifice is complete.

4. The Altar of Sacrifice (Genesis 22:9–12)

Perhaps the most famous altar in Abraham's life is the one on Mount Moriah—where he laid his promised son before the Lord.

This altar wasn't about death—it was about trust. Abraham believed that God could raise Isaac if necessary (Hebrews 11:19). And so, he held nothing back. Not even the promise.

This is where many in the Church struggle. We withhold what's most precious—our ambitions, relationships, and comfort zones—and call it wisdom. But God is still asking, "Will you lay it down?"

We can't experience resurrection power without experiencing the altar of sacrifice.

Abraham's altars were not religious monuments. They were markers of total consecration.

If we are to rebuild what has been lost in the American Church, we must start here. Not with better branding or strategy. But with lives laid bare before the Lord—with altars that cost us something.

Because the altar is the place where self dies…
…and where revival begins.

Abraham vs. Lot — Consecration vs. Compromise

When Abraham and Lot parted ways in Genesis 13, it was far more than a land dispute—it was a spiritual divergence, a fork in the road that revealed the true condition of their hearts. And the consequences of their choices would ripple into generations.

Strife had broken out between their herdsmen due to their growing wealth. In a gesture of humility and maturity, Abraham—who had every right to choose first—offered Lot the opportunity to take whichever portion of land he preferred. Rather than defer or pray, Lot lifted up his eyes and chose what looked best.

*"Lot lifted up his eyes and saw all the valley of the Jordan,
that it was well watered everywhere… like the garden of the Lord,
like the land of Egypt…"* — **Genesis 13:10 NASB**

That last phrase should've raised alarm: like the land of Egypt. Egypt symbolized past bondage. Yet Lot was drawn to it. He wasn't seeking spiritual covering—he was chasing material abundance, seduced by what appeared fertile and promising.

Lot walked by sight. Abraham walked by faith.

After Lot departed, Abraham didn't scramble to secure territory or retaliate. He simply worshiped.

*"Then Abram moved his tent and came and dwelt by the oaks of
Mamre, which are in Hebron, and there he built an altar to the Lord."*
— Genesis 13:18 NASB

Abraham chose Mamre, a name that means "fatness" or "strength." But he didn't choose it based on what his eyes could see—he chose it by trusting the God who had called him. And instead of building toward self, Abraham built an altar—a declaration of surrender and gratitude.

Lot, on the other hand, pitched his tent near Sodom—a place already notorious for its wickedness (Genesis 13:12-13). It wasn't long before he wasn't just near Sodom, he was living in it. And by Genesis 19, he was calling its depraved men "brothers," offering them his daughters to protect his guests.

That's what compromise does—it rewires your discernment and deforms your convictions.

The Fruit of Their Choices

Here's what unfolded after their paths diverged:

Lot's story became one of spiritual regression:

- He lost his wife, who looked back longingly at Sodom and was turned to salt.

- His daughters, poisoned by Sodom's ways, intoxicated him and committed incest.

- The result? The birth of Moab and Ammon—two nations that would become thorns in Israel's side.

- He left Sodom physically, but the Sodom mentality never left his family.

- Lot escaped with his life—but lost nearly everything else: his legacy, moral authority, spiritual clarity, and even his dignity.

Abraham's story, by contrast, blossomed:

- God reaffirmed and expanded His covenant with Abraham (Genesis 15).

- He received supernatural promises and became a friend of God.

- His faith was credited as righteousness, and his obedience gave birth to Isaac, the son of promise.

- He became the father of many nations, a patriarch of faith for Jews and Gentiles alike.

Abraham's altar-building lifestyle became the very foundation for divine legacy. Lot's tent-pitching near sin led to moral collapse.

Two paths, two very different legacies.

Here is the sobering comparison:

Abraham	Lot
Walked by faith and chose Mamre	Walked by sight and chose Sodom
Built altars to the Lord	Pitched tents near sin
Dwelt in the land of promise	Moved into a land of perversion
Interceded for the lost	Became compromised by their ways
Legacy of faith	Legacy of confusion

This is the tragic plight of the American Christian: *We want all the benefits of righteousness, but without paying the cost of consecration.* We want to pitch our tents near the world, yet walk in the favor of Abraham. We want revival without repentance. In doing so, many have wandered far from the promises of God while still attending church and lifting hands in worship.

We cannot live in Lot's tent and inherit Abraham's reward.

We cannot flirt with Sodom and expect Hebron's peace. The choice is set before us again: build altars or pitch tents. One invites glory. The other invites grief.

Transition Paragraph:

Before we can repair the altar and reclaim what has been defiled, we must identify the forces responsible for its desecration. It's not enough to rebuke sin in general—we must expose the spirits behind the compromise, confusion, and corruption that have infiltrated the house of God. Chief among them is a dark power the Bible has not left unnamed: Jezebel. Her ancient influence lives on today, working behind pulpits, in pews, and in our personal lives—undermining godly authority and seducing the people of God into spiritual adultery. As we move into the next section, we will pull back the curtain on this insidious spirit and equip the saints to confront her with holy boldness and uncompromising truth.

End-of-Chapter Review Questions

1. In what ways have modern Christians mimicked Lot's decision-making process—choosing by sight rather than by faith?

_____

_____

2. Why is altar-building (spiritually speaking) still essential for believers today? What does it represent in the life of a Christian?

_____

_____

3. How does the cultural embrace of syncretism ("coexistence" of beliefs) subtly erode biblical truth in the Church?

_____

_____

4. What warning signs from Lot's story should the American Church take seriously today?

_____

_____

5. Where have you personally been tempted to "pitch your tent near Sodom"? How can you reposition yourself like Abraham at Mamre?

_____

_____

6. How do worship trends, media influence, or celebrity culture contribute to modern-day spiritual mixture?

_____

_____

7. What would it look like for the Church in America to choose Abraham's path of faith, even when it means loss or discomfort in the short term?

_____

_____

8. Why is yoga considered spiritually dangerous according to its origins?

_____

_____

9. How does Halloween violate the spirit of holiness God desires?

_____

_____

10. How are we to deal with transgres sions of witchcraft in our lives? What ways has witchcraft insidiously crept into your life? What will you do to get rid of it in your life?

_____

_____

Know Thy Enemy

"We are not fighting against people made of flesh and blood, but against persons without bodies—the evil rulers of the unseen world, those mighty satanic beings and great evil princes of darkness who rule this world." —**Ephesians 6:12 (TLB)**

The Nature of the Enemy

The spiritual conflict facing the Church is not metaphorical—it is a very real war. In order to stand firm, believers must understand their adversaries and the spiritual hierarchy they operate within. Among the most cunning and destructive forces at work in the Church today is the Jezebel spirit. Although I mentioned this spirit briefly in the last chapter I thought it would be good to arm you with more details about it and the other spirits it runs with and reigns over. Demons are like wolves in that they hunt in packs. They're almost never solo.

So if there's a Jezebel spirit operating in your church or in your life, you can be sure these other spirits will be there causing trouble as well.

"The greatest enemies to revival are not outside the Church—they're operating from within." —**Lester Sumrall**

The Jezebel spirit, named after the infamous queen of Israel, embodies seduction, manipulation, idolatry, and rebellion against God's order. This spirit is not gendered—it can operate through men or women— but it functions through the traits first exemplified in Queen Jezebel's biblical story.

"You must understand spiritual hierarchy. Demons do."
—Rebecca Brown, MD, He Came to Set the Captives Free

Spiritual Rank and Domain 101

In the satanic hierarchy, Jezebel is often considered a ruling principality. She operates under Satan's broader kingdom and often partners with spirits of:

- Control & Manipulation
- Witchcraft & Divination
- Lust & Seduction
- Pride & Rebellion
- Offense & Bitterness
- Religious Hypocrisy

She is often accompanied by an Ahab spirit, which enables her by forfeiting godly authority. This dynamic is particularly dangerous within churches where leadership lacks boldness and conviction.

"Jezebel seeks to kill the prophets of God. She hates authority that exposes her." **—Rebecca Brown, MD**

The Book of Revelation speaks directly of this spirit:

"But I have this against you, that you tolerate that woman Jezebel, who calls herself a prophetess and teaches and leads My bond-servants astray so that they commit sexual immorality and eat things sacrificed to idols." **—Revelation 2:20 (NASB)**

Methods of Operation

Jezebel is rarely obvious. Her weapons are subtlety, flattery, intimidation, and manipulation cloaked in spiritual language. She draws people into relationships built on loyalty to her rather than to Christ. Her goal is always to usurp authority, silence the voice of true prophets, and corrupt pure worship.

"Jezebel's goal is always control. She operates in the shadows but pulls the strings." —**Lester Sumrall**

"The Jezebel spirit uses half-truths, counterfeit love, and prophetic manipulation to gain influence. She hates repentance and refuses correction." —**Rebecca Brown, MD**

Signs of Jezebel's Influence in the Church

- A culture of fear and passivity among leadership
- Tolerance of sin and compromise to keep the peace
- Suppression of prophetic voices
- Strong personalities usurping spiritual authority
- Seduction of believers into emotional or sexual entanglements under a religious guise

"If Satan can't destroy a church with persecution, he'll corrupt it from within through Jezebel." —**Lester Sumrall**

Combating Jezebel

The only effective response to this spirit is:

- Deep personal holiness
- Unwavering submission to the Lordship of Christ
- Bold, Spirit-led leadership
- Fasting and prayer
- Swift rejection of false teaching and manipulation

"Spiritual warfare isn't shouting into the air. It's walking in holiness and obedience. That's what Jezebel fears most." —**Rebecca Brown, MD**

Jezebel's final judgment was declared by God Himself. As foretold in 2 Kings 9:33, she was thrown down and devoured by dogs—a grotesque but sobering reminder that no principality will ultimately escape God's wrath.

"And he said, 'Throw her down.' So they threw her down,
and some of her blood splattered on the wall and on the horses,
and he trampled her underfoot." —**2 Kings 9:33 (NKJV)**

May the Church never forget the danger of tolerating what God has condemned.

Transition Paragraph:

The veil has now been pulled back. We've exposed the Jezebel spirit and the demonic kingdom she operates within—highlighting the deception, seduction, and rebellion she inspires. But knowing your enemy is only the beginning. The next step requires self-examination and obedience. Many believers unknowingly invite spiritual defilement into their homes and churches by clinging to things the Lord has called "accursed." Whether through ignorance, rebellion, or misplaced sentiment, these hidden objects serve as legal ground for the enemy to oppress, harass, and hinder God's people. In the next chapter, we'll uncover the biblical account of Achan's disobedience and explore the spiritual dangers of harboring cursed objects. This isn't just about things—it's about alignment, obedience, and spiritual authority.

End-of-Chapter Review Questions

1. What are the defining characteristics of the Jezebel spirit, and how do they manifest in both individuals and church systems today?

    _____

    _____

2. How does the Jezebel spirit wage war against godly order, and what role does Ahab's passivity play in empowering her influence?

    _____

    _____

3. According to Lester Sumrall and Rebecca Brown, why is it critical for believers to recognize and confront the Jezebel spirit rather than tolerate it? Include insights from their quotes and how those ideas connect to biblical examples.

    _____

    _____

4. How does understanding the Jezebel spirit help Christians walk in spiritual authority and dominion on the earth?

    _____

    _____

5. In what ways does the Church today tolerate the influence of Jezebel, and how can believers practically 'throw her down' as Jehu did?

    _____

    _____

Stop Hiding Achan's Accursed Objects

Cursed Objects, Demonic Attachments, and the Sin of Achan

A Spiritual Warfare Perspective

When Achan stole items from the ruins of Jericho, he wasn't just disobeying an order — he was introducing cursed objects into a holy camp. As a result, the favor of God lifted from Israel, and the nation suffered defeat (Joshua 7:1–5).

But why was God's reaction so severe?

The answer lies in what Jericho represented and the spiritual defilement associated with its possessions.

Who Were the People of Jericho?

Jericho was a Canaanite stronghold, a city known for its allegiance to false gods and its deeply embedded occult practices. God had declared Jericho to be under the ḥērem — devoted to destruction — because of the abominations practiced there:

- Baal and Asherah worship, which included ritual prostitution and sexual perversion

- Child sacrifice to Molech (Leviticus 18:21; Deuteronomy 12:31)

- Sorcery, divination, and necromancy (Deuteronomy 18:9–12)

The possessions of these people weren't neutral. They were tools of demonic worship and instruments of spiritual bondage.

51

"But as for you, only keep yourselves from the things under the ban, so that you do not covet them and take some of the things under the ban, and turn the camp of Israel into something cursed and bring disaster on it." - **Joshua 6:18 (NASB):**

Demons and Cursed Objects

Throughout Scripture and spiritual experience, it is evident that demons attach themselves to objects that were:

- Used in ritual worship of false gods
- Dedicated to occult or pagan practices
- Handled in satanic ceremonies or consecrated to idols

These items act as spiritual doorways, giving legal ground for demonic presence.

"You must not bring any of the accursed objects into your home, lest the curse of destruction be upon you too, like it. You must utterly detest it and shun it, for it is cursed." - Deuteronomy 7:26 (TLB):

Quotes from Renowned Deliverance Ministers

(Derek Prince)

"Anything associated with idolatry or the occult — even if it seems harmless — can bring a curse into your life if you take it into your home." **— Blessing or Curse: You Can Choose,**

"Don't be deceived. Objects can carry spiritual power. If it has been used in the service of Satan, it will carry his imprint." **— They Shall Expel Demons**

(Rebecca Brown, M.D.)

"Satanists know that objects used in rituals can carry demons. When such objects are given to unsuspecting Christians, it gives the demons legal ground to attack." — **He Came to Set the Captives Free**

"Many Christians suffer torment in their homes and bodies because they have brought cursed items inside — jewelry, statues, books, music. You must destroy them completely." — **Prepare for War**

(Lester Sumrall)

"Demons are legalists. If you give them a right of way — even through an object — they will enter." — **Alien Entities**

"Every missionary knows that idol worship opens the door to demon power. Remove the idol, and the demon loses its grip." — **Demons: The Answer Book**

Achan's Theft: A Warning for Today

When Achan stole the Babylonian garment, the silver, and the gold bar, he didn't just steal wealth — he stole defiled items, likely dedicated to false gods. His hidden sin brought judgment upon all of Israel until it was exposed and removed.

"There is an accursed thing in your midst, O Israel. You cannot stand before your enemies until you remove it." - **Joshua 7:13 (NASB):**

Today, many believers unknowingly bring cursed items into their homes:

- Statues of deities, figurines related to witchcraft (i.e.., any Manga, Dragonball Z, Pokemon or Harry Potter toys, etc.)
- Crystals or "healing stones"
- Books or jewelry linked to occult themes

- "Souvenirs" from temples, pagan cultures, or witchcraft
- Any objects related to Christmas, Easter, or Halloween
- Any objects related to dragons, Star Wars, or the like

These may appear harmless — but spiritually, they grant the enemy access into your life... even if you are a professing Christian.

By harboring these forbidden items in your tent, you have unwittingly granted these demons spiritual authority to enter your life and to hinder and rob you of God's blessings (peace, joy, abundant health, anointing, unity in your marriage and family, your masculinity, your femininity, etc.). Until you repent and rid your home of these accursed objects you will not be able to stand before your enemies just like Israel. We must stop accepting any and everything the Devil drops off at our doorstep!

Defeat, drama, damaged relationships, poverty, so called "bad luck", and impaired health (*take medical recommendations yes, but also stand on God's promises and expect them to manifest in your life*). Stop accepting these and every other stressful thing that comes your way as normal.

We must learn how to fight spiritually and how to use the spiritual weapons that God gave us.

> *"...lest Satan should take advantage of us; for we are not ignorant of his devices."* — **2 Corinthians 2:11, NKJV**

> *"Behold, I give unto you power to tread on serpents and scorpions, and over all the power of the enemy: and nothing shall by any means hurt you."* — **Luke 10:19, KJV**

Look at Luke 10:19, the "I" refers to the Lord. The "you" refers to you. In other words, God gave ***you*** the power to walk in victory over all of the power of the Devil. Repent. Pursue holiness. Learn how to walk in the power of the Holy Spirit and take back what the Devil has stolen from you in your life.

Final Thought

God is holy. As such, He commands His people to be holy: spiritually clean, not just morally upright. We must examine our homes and hearts, ensuring we've not allowed the enemy a foothold through accursed objects.

"... and do not give the devil a foothold." -Ephesians 4:27 NIV:

The word translated as "place" or "foothold" comes from the Greek word topos, which literally means a location, position, or room. Paul is warning believers ("YOU") not to leave open spiritual space for the devil to operate in — through unrepentant sin, anger, bitterness, or (as in the context we're discussing) cursed objects or disobedience. Choose holiness. Get rid of that accursed object and walk in the freedom, power and victory that Jesus won for you on the cross!

Transition Paragraph

The tragedy of hidden sins and spiritual compromise is that they often remain unchallenged when they masquerade as harmless tradition or cultural norm. As we've seen, even one accursed object can open the door to destruction. But what happens when an entire nation — even God's people — celebrate days that are rooted in darkness and idolatry? In the next chapter, we pull back the curtain on seemingly innocent celebrations like Halloween and explore how Satan has cleverly repackaged the profane as playful. It's time to ask hard questions: Are we celebrating what God calls cursed? Are we dancing around altars He never ordained?

End-of-Chapter Review Questions

1. Why do you think God dealt so severely with Achan's sin in Joshua 7? What does this reveal about the seriousness of spiritual disobedience?

   _____

   _____

2. Have you ever brought something into your home without considering its spiritual origin? How can you begin discerning whether items may be spiritually harmful?

   _____

   _____

3. What are some modern examples of "accursed objects" that Christians may unknowingly harbor, and what are the consequences of doing so?

   _____

   _____

4. According to Scripture and the teachings of leaders like Derek Prince, Rebecca Brown, and Lester Sumrall, how do demons use physical objects as legal grounds for influence?

   _____

   _____

5. Are you willing to ask the Holy Spirit to reveal anything in your life, home, or heart that needs to be removed? What steps will you take to destroy any "accursed things" the Lord brings to your attention?

   _____

   _____

CHAPTER 3D

Unholy Holi-Days

"They worship me in vain; their teachings are merely human rules."
— Matthew 15:9 (NIV)

A False Light in Festive Garments

The enemy is a master of disguise—rarely revealing his true intent openly. Instead, he cloaks his deceptions in light, wrapping idolatry in ribbons and sacred-sounding traditions. Modern Christian observances such as Christmas, Easter, and Halloween, though celebrated with joy and community spirit, are deeply rooted in pagan rituals and ancient demonic customs. And for many in the body of Christ, the danger lies not in intentional rebellion, but in passive compromise disguised as tradition. These are the insidious ways the devil tricks Christians. The Oxford English Dictionary defines "insidious" *as a formal, disapproving adjective that describes something that spreads gradually or without being noticed, but causes serious harm.* Celebrating these widely practiced traditions as Christian, (or rebranding them) seems innocuous but causes us great harm without us even noticing. The scripture tells us:

"Surely, in vain the net is spread in the sight of any bird;"
— Proverbs 1:17, KJV

In other words, Satan's traps are NEVER obvious and will need to be spiritually discerned through the Holy Spirit. The Devil can't trick God's Holy Spirit like he can humans. Very often, he insidiously veils his dark things in religious veneer. If the Devil and his angels and demons disguise themselves as deities and angels, then it should be no surprise that they would cloak their demonic days of worship as something godly.

"And no wonder! For Satan himself transforms himself into an angel of light. Therefore it is no great thing if his ministers also transform themselves into ministers of righteousness, whose end will be according to their works." — **2 Corinthians 11:14–15, NKJV**

We must not be deceived by how we feel about a particular thing. This is how Satan deceives many Christians. We must learn how the Devil operates. We must learn how to fight spiritually and how to use the spiritual weapons that God gave us.

"…lest Satan should take advantage of us; for we are not ignorant of his devices." — **2 Corinthians 2:11, NKJV**

Pagan Roots of Christmas

The Word of God never commands us to celebrate the birth of Christ, nor does it suggest the date of December 25th. That date, however, was celebrated in Roman culture as the birthday of Sol Invictus—the unconquered sun. The winter solstice, marked by the rebirth of the sun in pagan belief systems, became a convenient date for the early Roman Catholic Church to "Christianize" existing sun god worship.

Scripture clearly warns against adopting pagan customs:

"Thus says the Lord: Do not learn the way of the nations… for the customs of the peoples are vanity. A tree from the forest is cut down and worked with an axe by the hands of a craftsman. They decorate it with silver and gold…" — Jeremiah 10:2–4 (ESV)

This passage describes practices eerily similar to the modern tradition of the Christmas tree—originally derived from Asherah pole worship and other fertility rites. As believers, we must ask: If the root is unholy, can the fruit be holy?

Easter: A Name Worth Questioning

The term "Easter" itself is derived from Eostre, the Anglo-Saxon goddess of fertility and spring. The eggs, rabbits, and sunrise services have more in common with pagan spring festivals than with the resurrection of Jesus Christ. While the resurrection is worthy of daily reverence, the syncretism of holy remembrance with fertility symbols is not.

> *"You cannot drink the cup of the Lord and the cup of demons too; you cannot have a part in both the Lord's table and the table of demons."*
> **— 1 Corinthians 10:21 (NIV)**

1. Eostre / Ishtar – The Pagan Origins

Eostre (Anglo-Saxon) or Ostara (Germanic) was a goddess of spring, fertility, and rebirth. Her symbols included eggs (fertility) and rabbits (rapid reproduction).Similarly, the ancient Babylonian goddess Ishtar was associated with fertility, love, war, and rebirth. Her rites included sacred prostitution, and her resurrection myths often involved the underworld—paralleling seasonal cycles of life and death.

2. Resurrection Sunday: The Biblical Account

Jesus Christ rose from the dead on the first day of the week following Passover (see Luke 24:1, John 20:1). Early Christians celebrated this event with no reference to Eostre, rabbits, or eggs. They observed Resurrection Sunday or First Fruits, closely tied to Passover, as commanded in the Jewish calendar (Leviticus 23:9–14).

3. Syncretism Under the Roman Church

As Christianity spread across pagan Europe, the Roman Church intentionally absorbed local traditions to make conversion easier. The name "Easter" (used in English and German) was adopted in place of Pesach (Passover) to align with existing pagan spring festivals. Fertility symbols like eggs and rabbits were incorporated into the church calendar—not from Scripture, but from pagan tradition.

Why This Matters

The resurrection of Jesus is central to the Christian faith (1 Cor 15:14), yet attaching it to pagan fertility celebrations distorts its holy meaning. God commands His people not to mix holy with unholy:

"What fellowship can light have with darkness?"
– 2 Corinthians 6:14

"Stop accepting the Devil's lies about what the Lord gave you and what He didn't! Stop playing with the Devil in the sandbox and letting him walk off with your stuff!" — **Michael M. Dillard**

Halloween: A Celebration of Death

Halloween has perhaps the clearest association with demonic origins. Known as Samhain in Celtic tradition, October 31 marked a day when the veil between the living and the dead was thinnest—prompting offerings to appease spirits and demonic forces. The practice of dressing in costumes originated from fear of spiritual retaliation.

The Lord commands us to be holy and set apart. Participating in a holiday rooted in necromancy, death, and fear is not merely cultural— it's covenantal compromise. Rebranding Halloween as Harvest Festivals, Trunk-or-Treat events, and Bible-themed costume parties will not change what the holiday actually is. It will not change the demonic roots of what is being celebrated and even invited to come in to your midst. Think about this: when did you ever read in the Holy Bible about Jesus taking a pagan practice and changing its name to make it more acceptable to those that were perishing? I know that you are having a difficult time calling a scripture to mind. That's because it never happened. Jesus (who is the visible representation of the Invisible God) would NEVER do such a thing. Or tell His followers to do such wicked things. These are all man-based, doctrines of demons that have nothing at all to do with Jesus the Christ. Just because you say they do doesn't mean that they actually do. Just because you attach God's name to it doesn't mean He has anything to do with it whatsoever. Think about the number of worldly musicians (rock stars, R & B singers and rappers) who accept music awards and say they want to thank God for making it happen for them. The Lord has nothing to do with them being in that wicked industry and singing those wicked songs. It is exactly the same with Christmas, Easter and Trunk or Treat. The Lord is __*not*__ in it regardless of how much you say He is.

The Error of Assimilation: Paganism and the Saints

The early Roman Catholic Church often assimilated regional pagan deities into its calendar by renaming them as "saints." For example, the goddess Brigid of Ireland became "Saint Brigid." Shrines were renamed, idols repurposed, and pagan festivals rebranded. This pattern of compromise became the foundation for much of what we now call "Christian tradition."

> *"They did not destroy the peoples as the Lord had commanded them,*
> *but they mingled with the nations and adopted their customs."*
> **— Psalm 106:34–35 (NIV)**

The assimilation of idols was not reformation—it was contamination.

New Moons, Feasts, and False Religion

The Lord often rebuked Israel for keeping religious feasts without true repentance.

> *"Stop bringing meaningless offerings! Your incense is detestable to me.*
> *New Moons, Sabbaths and convocations—I cannot bear your worthless*
> *assemblies."* **— Isaiah 1:13 (NIV)**

Modern holidays that mix truth and error fall into the same category. God does not delight in festivities performed in His name but rooted in rebellion. True worship begins with obedience and holiness, not pageantry.

Transition Paragraph:

As we uncover the sinister roots behind the holidays many Christians celebrate without question, a sobering truth emerges—our altars have been compromised, and our worship diluted. But the problem runs deeper than decorations and dates. It's not merely what we celebrate, but how we live. In a nation where Christian vernacular is fluent but obedience is scarce, the Lord's warning echoes louder than ever: "Why do you call Me, 'Lord, Lord,' and do not do what I say?" (Luke 6:46). It is time we confront the uncomfortable questions that separate true disciples from cultural Christians.

Let us now turn the page to examine the words of Christ Himself and ask: Do we truly know Him—or are we merely performing in His name?

End-of-Chapter Reflection Questions

1. How has learning the origins of holidays like Christmas, Easter, and Halloween challenged your understanding of what is acceptable worship?

_____

_____

2. Have you or your church unknowingly embraced syncretism— mixing holy and pagan elements? If so, what will you do about it?

_____

_____

3. Read Jeremiah 10:1–5. How does this passage influence your view on Christmas trees and other seasonal customs?

_____

_____

4. What do you believe God desires most from His people in worship—cultural conformity or consecrated obedience? Why?

_____

_____

5. What steps can you take to ensure your household does not bring accursed objects or practices into alignment with demonic influence?

_____

_____

CHAPTER 4

Lord, Lord!
Asking Yourself the Tough Questions

"The greatest tragedy isn't that sinners go to hell—it's that many churchgoers think they're saved and won't realize they're lost until it's too late."
— **Michael M. Dillard**

For decades, American Christianity has trafficked in cheap assurance—offering promises of salvation with little demand for transformation. The modern altar call often centers on personal comfort, not covenant surrender. We've built sanctuaries full of professing believers, but far fewer disciples. And tragically, some of the most sobering words in all of Scripture are aimed not at the atheist or pagan, but at the one who thinks they're already in.

"Not everyone who says to Me, 'Lord, Lord,' shall enter the kingdom of heaven, but he who does the will of My Father in heaven."
— **Matthew 7:21 (NKJV)**

Jesus doesn't rebuke the irreligious in this passage—He rebukes the religiously active. These are people who prophesy, cast out demons, and perform miracles in His name. Yet He declares, *"I never knew you. Depart from Me, you who practice lawlessness."* The implication is chilling: It's possible to be outwardly active in ministry and yet inwardly estranged from Christ.

This chapter is a call to holy introspection. It's time to ask ourselves—and the American Church—some hard, uncomfortable, but absolutely necessary questions. Because eternity hangs in the balance, and Jesus isn't coming back for a crowd—He's returning for a Bride.

Walking in the Light

Many today claim to know God, but walk in darkness—a contradiction that Scripture does not tolerate. The apostle John draws a hard line between fellowship with God and our actual conduct:

> *"If we say we have fellowship with Him and walk in darkness, we lie and do not practice the truth."* — **1 John 1:6 (NKJV)**

The tragic plight of the American Christian is that many have redefined darkness. Pornography is "personal struggle." Homosexuality is "an alternative lifestyle." Gossip is "venting." Greed is "grind." Pride is "self-care." We have rebranded sin, and in doing so, nullified repentance.

John continues:

> *"But if we walk in the light as He is in the light, we have fellowship with one another, and the blood of Jesus Christ His Son cleanses us from all sin."* — **1 John 1:7 (NKJV)**

Notice the order: Walk in the light → enjoy fellowship → experience cleansing. There's no cleansing for those who hide. There's no healing for those who fake holiness. The blood of Jesus isn't a cover for habitual rebellion; it's a cleansing for those who choose exposure and truth.

What Does It Mean to Walk in the Light?

To walk in the light is not to walk in perfection but in exposure—in truth, in honesty, in accountability. It means to live openly before God, not hiding in shadows or rationalizations. This is where authentic transformation begins—not in emotional church experiences, but in sustained surrender.

Charles Spurgeon once said,

"A religion that never suffices to govern a man's behavior will never save his soul."

Many churches today have replaced the light of the gospel with stage lights and smoke machines, offering theatrical experiences instead of transformative truth. We've given people a reason to feel good on Sunday without equipping them to live holy on Monday.

The result? Spiritual delusion. People believe they are fine because they "felt something" at church or serve in ministry. But the fruit of their lives—bitterness, sexual immorality, compromise, spiritual laziness—tells a different story.

> *"Now by this we know that we know Him, if we keep His commandments. He who says, 'I know Him,' and does not keep His commandments, is a liar, and the truth is not in him."*
> **— 1 John 2:3–4 (NKJV)**

This is not a message of condemnation—it's a wake-up call. We must return to measuring our Christianity by Scripture, not by feelings, cultural trends, or online sermons. Walking in the light will cost us something—it exposes us, humbles us, and transforms us. But that's where true fellowship and power begin.

A Personal Testimony: Broken, But Not Abandoned

In 2008, my spiritual life, family life, and work life were in complete disarray. I was selfish, easily irritable, and emotionally closed off. I seemed to be constantly in conflict—whether upsetting my wife at the time, provoking my children to anger (sometimes intentionally, other times not), or landing in trouble at work.

Yet somehow, we maintained the practice of holding family Bible study each weeknight after dinner. The kids weren't exactly thrilled about it, but they showed up.

One night, as I opened in prayer, a piercing scripture was read aloud. As it landed in the room, we all knew without question—it was a direct rebuke from the Lord, and it was meant for me.

I was devastated. Everything in me wanted to break down right there, but I tried to hold my composure. When the study ended and everyone went to bed, I stayed downstairs. I wept. I prayed. My heart had just been shattered by the Word of God. The Holy Spirit made it clear: God was displeased with me. And He was absolutely right.

I had allowed my flesh to lead me into patterns of disobedience, and my family was paying the price. That night, I pleaded with the Lord to forgive me—to change me—to help me live a life that was righteous, not just religious. I thought no one else had heard my cries, but years later, my youngest daughter told me she remembered hearing me crying that night.

Although it's painful to realize there's a gap between how God sees us and how we see ourselves, it is far better to be broken and corrected on this side of eternity than to hear those chilling words from Jesus:

"Away from Me, you evildoer. I never knew you."

The Fear of the Lord

The modern church has largely lost the fear of the Lord—and with it, the power that reverence once produced. In our pursuit of relevance and acceptance, we've made God overly familiar and comfortable. We talk about Him like a buddy, sing about Him like a boyfriend, and sometimes even treat Him like a divine vending machine—insert your tithe, select your blessing.

But Scripture paints a far more sobering picture:

"The Lord takes pleasure in those who fear Him, in those who hope in His mercy." — **Psalm 147:11 (NKJV)**

To fear the Lord is not to tremble in dread of abuse—it is to stand in awe of His holiness, His justice, and His unapproachable majesty. It is to recognize that this God we serve is a consuming fire, not a cosmic pushover. The fear of the Lord is foundational to wisdom (Prov. 9:10), to turning from evil (Prov. 16:6), and to lasting obedience (Eccl. 12:13).

Yet, the American Church has adopted a casual tone that breeds carelessness. God is approached with flip-flops and a latte, not with contrition and reverence. And the results speak for themselves: sin is winked at, holiness is optional, and repentance is rare.

Charles Stanley once warned,

*"The fear of the Lord is the beginning of obedience. Without it, we reduce God to a God of our own making—one who is expected to tolera*te everything and judge nothing."

Many of today's Christians walk in open rebellion yet wonder why their prayers go unanswered, why their homes lack peace, and why their spiritual lives are barren. Could it be that they've never known the God who causes men to fall as dead at His feet?

We forget that it was fear of the Lord that gripped the early Church in Acts 5, when Ananias and Sapphira dropped dead after lying to the Holy Spirit. This wasn't the Old Testament—this was post-resurrection, New Covenant Christianity! And yet, God demonstrated that He does not play games with hypocrisy.

"Great fear came upon all the church and upon all who heard these things." **— Acts 5:11 (NKJV)**

If that kind of fear were present in our churches today, how many worship leaders would fall silent? How many preachers would step down? How many churchgoers would flee the altar instead of flocking to it?

We don't tremble because we don't understand who He is. We don't understand who He is because we don't really know Him. And we don't know Him because, at the root, we've lost the reverent fear that opens the door to relationship.

The fear of the Lord is not an enemy to love—it's the evidence of it. Only those who understand His greatness will long to live in a way that honors Him. It is the fear of the Lord that keeps us from sin, reminds us of accountability, and preserves us in a world of compromise. It is the fear of the Lord that reminds us He is God—and we are not.

Transition Paragraph:

The call to examine ourselves isn't rooted in guilt or shame—but in mercy. Jesus lovingly warns us so we will not be caught off guard at the Judgment. The words "Lord, Lord" on the lips of the unrepentant are not a cry of love, but a plea of presumption. To avoid becoming part of that tragic chorus, we must allow the Spirit of God to convict us now—while there is still time to walk in the light, come out from Babylon, and grow in holy fear. The gospel that was preached by Jesus and the apostles was not a self-help manual—it was a call to die to self and live to God. And so we now turn to that very message—the Gospel They Never Preached.

End-of-Chapter Review Questions

1. According to Matthew 7:21–23, what is the danger of calling Jesus "Lord" while living in disobedience?

   _____

   _____

2. How do the Scriptures define genuine love for God, and how does that contrast with cultural definitions of love?

   _____

   _____

3. Reflecting on your own walk: are there areas of disobedience or self-deception that need to be surrendered to Christ today?

_____

_____

4. How does 2 Timothy 2:19 affirm the idea that salvation produces visible fruit in a believer's life?

_____

_____

5. What is the difference between godly sorrow and worldly sorrow? Why is this distinction critical to true repentance?

_____

_____

6. How did the fear of the Lord impact the early Church in Acts 5, and what might that look like in today's churches?

_____

_____

7. In what ways have modern church environments possibly dulled our sense of reverence for God?

_____

_____

8. How can personal or corporate revival begin with a renewed fear of the Lord?

_____

_____

9. What lessons can we draw from Michael's testimony of conviction and transformation? Have you had a similar experience with the Holy Spirit and what was the outcome for your life?

_____

_____

10. What changes might the Holy Spirit be asking you to make in response to this chapter?

_____

_____

CHAPTER 5

The Gospel They Never Preached

"But the king said to Araunah, 'No, but I will buy it from you for a price. I will not offer burnt offerings to the LORD my God that cost me nothing.'"
- 2 Samuel 24:24 (ESV)

Introduction

Across churches in America, a different gospel is being preached—one that speaks often of love but rarely of lordship, that elevates grace while downplaying repentance, that promises heaven but neglects to warn of hell. It is soft, sweet, and seeker-friendly instead of sobering. And tragically, it is not the gospel of Jesus Christ at all.

This gospel being preached across America today costs believers nothing, demands nothing of them, and promises them everything. It promises salvation without surrender, blessing without brokenness, and Heaven without holiness. While it is popular, persuasive, and packed with emotionally stirring sermons and music—it is not the gospel that Jesus or His apostles preached. This diluted message has created generations of spiritually-deformed Christians who identify with Christ but do not walk in His ways. They claim salvation yet refuse surrender. They attend church but have never truly died to self. The result? A nation full of churchgoers who believe they are saved—but have never actually met the Savior. A nation full of churchgoing idolaters--essentially fiends in sheep's clothing. And this too is the tragic plight of the American Christian, we are blissfully unawares of our true spiritual position in relation to the Lord.

The modern church has, in many ways, exchanged the piercing call to die to self for a message that coddles the carnal man and tickles the ear. It proclaims comfort over conviction and speaks more about dreams and destiny than sin and sanctification. But the true gospel, as modeled by Christ, was never intended to be popular. It was always designed to be counter-cultural. It was always designed to be a cross.

> *"If anyone would come after me, let him deny himself and take up his cross daily and follow me."* —**Luke 9:23 (ESV)**

And this is the gospel today's popular churches never preach: Jesus didn't come to make any of us better, happier, and wealthier versions of ourselves. He came to kill the old man and raise up a new creation. Amen! The gospel is not an invitation to self-fulfillment; it is a call to die to one's inherently selfish nature.

The "death of self" is not metaphorical fluff—it is the very foundation of true discipleship.

In today's American Christian landscape, the altar has been replaced by the stage. Confession of one's transgressions has been replaced with positive affirmations. Denial of self has been replaced by self-expression. And the result? A generation of professing Christians who believe they can follow Jesus without forsaking the world and its ungodly ways.

But the words of Jesus still ring out with eternal weight and clarity:

> *"Whoever does not bear his own cross and come after me cannot be my disciple."* —**Luke 14:27 (ESV)**

We cannot belong to Christ and remain married to the culture. We cannot serve two masters—yet the modern gospel has convinced many that we can. That God will understand.

That grace will cover continual compromise. That fruitless belief is still belief.

This deception is as old as Eden.

The serpent didn't deny God's existence; he simply distorted His words. And Eve didn't place enough weight and importance on God's words to commit them exactly to memory.

He offered her a version of God's truth that was easier to swallow—just enough truth to seem safe, just enough poison to actually kill.

And that's exactly what's happening in our churches today.
What we're calling "grace" is often no more than a license to sin.
What we're calling "freedom" is often outright spiritual rebellion against the Lord.
What we're calling "inclusivity" is often the human erasure of God's holy and divine standards regarding the mixing of that which is clean with the unclean, man-based, doctrines of demons as it were.

But the true gospel never bowed to culture. It confronted it. It exposed darkness, uprooted idolatry, and turned the entire world upside down. That gospel had power. It had weight. It produced transformation. And it called men and women out of the darkness of their sin and into the marvelous light that accompanies holiness.

The time has come to return to this gospel that they've never preached. The one that costs everything—but gives far more than this world ever could.

The Call to Holiness

The gospel that Jesus preached was never soft. It did not stroke the ego or coddle the carnal nature. It was a blazing fire that called for repentance, separation, and total surrender of one's rights and the things their hearts most prized. It demanded that men and women die to themselves daily, not merely agree to a set of religious facts or praying a comfortable prayer at the altar and then checking the box on their spiritual checklist. Yet somewhere along the way, the American Church replaced that gospel with a soft, seeker-friendly substitute—complete with a non-holy, Barney-like Jesus who demands nothing of them. This imaginary god, crafted by their own flesh, permits them to live as they please and still promises Heaven without paying the price. It is a counterfeit doctrine of comfort built upon a foundation of deception and delusion.

Once again, we see the tragic plight of the American Christian: a people who expect eternal reward to be served on a silver platter, yet are unwilling to pay the high price that true holiness demands.

In Luke 14:26–27, Jesus plainly states:

"If anyone comes to me and does not hate father and mother, wife and children, brothers and sisters—yes, even their own life—such a person cannot be my disciple. And whoever does not carry their cross and follow me cannot be my disciple."

These are not suggestions or exaggerations. They are kingdom terms. They are non-negotiable and absolute. And they directly confront the modern American Christian's desire to follow Jesus on their own terms. In many churches, the very concept of "holiness" is now considered archaic, legalistic, or unloving.

The call for holiness barely makes its way into sermons, small groups, or discipleship curriculums. To be holy means to be set apart.

It means we cannot walk like the world, talk like the world, think like the world, or value what the world values. This means we do not celebrate and lift our voices in song to worldly music that does not glorify the Most High God and His values. This means we do not celebrate Halloween's wickedness or Harry Potter and his legacy of witchcraft that many Christians knowingly adopt and celebrate. This means we love the things that the Lord loves and we hate the things that He hates. It means we don't give the appearance of evil. If we look just like the world and are doing the same things the world is doing then we have a serious problem. And also, what is the incentive for non-believers to leave the world for

Christianity if there seems to be no difference? God's way is the more excellent way.

And holiness is not just a trait—it is the very character of God.
And Scripture tells us in Hebrews 12:14:
"Pursue peace with all people, and holiness, without which no one will see the Lord."

Not "good intentions," not "positive vibes," not even "church attendance"—but ___holiness___. Set-apartness. Moral purity. A life inherently and visibly different from the world.

This call to holiness was not just for the prophets or apostles; it is for every believer. Yet tragically, many American Christians reject this call because they have been discipled by culture, and not by Christ. We chase comfort over conviction, relevance over righteousness, and social approval over sanctification. We've traded in the true worship experience of being awed in God's presence for worldly pop and rap music thinly veiled with Christian references, smoke machines and flashy stage lights.

But the result is a Church that is largely indistinguishable from the world it's supposed to transform and it lacks the power of the Holy Spirit because He has departed the premises. It reminds me of 1 Samuel 4:17-22:

So the messenger answered and said, "Israel has fled before the Philistines, and there has been a great slaughter among the people. Also your two sons, Hophni and Phinehas, are dead; and the ark of God has been captured."

Then it happened, when he made mention of the ark of God, that Eli fell off the seat backward by the side of the gate; and his neck was broken and he died, for the man was old and heavy. And he had judged Israel forty years.

Now his daughter-in-law, Phinehas' wife, was with child, due to be delivered; and when she heard the news that the ark of God was captured, and that her father-in-law and her husband were dead, she bowed herself and gave birth, for her labor pains came upon her. And about the time of her death the women who stood by her said to her, "Do not fear, for you have borne a son." But she did not answer, nor did she regard it. Then she named the child Ichabod, saying, "The glory has departed from Israel!" because the ark of God had been captured and because of her father-in-law and her husband. And she said, "The glory has departed from Israel, for the ark of God has been captured."

The Apostle Peter echoed the Lord's command for holiness in 1 Peter 1:15–16:

"But just as he who called you is holy, so be holy in all you do; for it is written: 'Be holy, because I am holy.'"

Holiness is not mere behavior modification. It is a supernatural transformation—a Holy Spirit-empowered lifestyle birthed from intimacy with the Lord. Yet it is not an automatic thing that every believer receives upon coming to Christ. It is cultivated. It is pursued.

It requires the intentional dying to our flesh, choosing daily obedience throughout the course of our lives, and a deeply abiding love for truth. Holiness is not about legalism; It's about valuing the presence of God so much that we gladly lay down anything that hinders it. The apostle Paul proclaimed in Philippians 3:8-9:

Yet indeed I also count all things loss for the excellence of the knowledge of Christ Jesus my Lord, for whom I have suffered the loss of all things, and count them as rubbish, that I may gain Christ and be found in Him, not having my own righteousness, which is from the law, but that which is through faith in Christ, the righteousness which is from God by faith;

In Philippians 3:8, the Greek word translated as "rubbish" is σκύβαλον (skubalon). While often rendered as "rubbish" or "garbage" in English, it more literally means "dung," "excrement," or "manure". Some translations even use the term "dung" for this verse.

In other words, after coming to Christ, Paul is saying that everything in his life he once held dear now held the same value as cow manure.

This powerful imagery emphasizes the intensity of Paul's conviction that knowing Christ and His holiness is far superior to any worldly achievement or gain. But far too many pulpits are afraid to offend churchgoers by talking about holy lifestyles vs the alternative lifestyles that are widely accepted by so many churches. So instead of preaching the full gospel they've settled for motivational speeches, personal development tips, and light doses of grace with no weight of accountability. Think about it. How many churches today consistently preach holiness, if at all?

How many pastors urge their congregants to crucify their flesh, flee immorality, not love the world or the things of the world, and to surrender everything for Christ? Instead, we are told: "Come as you are—and stay as you are. You don't have to stop your worldly practices. It's all about your level of personal conviction." This is not the gospel. This is a fine-sounding argument and self-deception. Jesus never promised us comfort. He promised us a cross. He never said we could keep our old lives. He said we must lose them:

For whoever desires to save his life will lose it, but whoever loses his life for My sake will find it. For what profit is it to a man if he gains the whole world, and loses his own soul? Or what will a man give in exchange for his soul? For the Son of Man will come in the glory of His Father with His angels, and then He will reward each according to his works.-- Matthew 16:25-27 NKJV

But we love our worldly practices, worldly music, worldly movies and worldly holidays. Therefore, we refuse to give up these things that we've come to love and value so much even if it means being distant from God. As the scripture says:

And this is the condemnation, that the light has come into the world, and men loved darkness rather than light, because their deeds were evil. -- John 3:19 NKJV

Jesus never said holiness was optional. He said, *"Be perfect, therefore, as your heavenly Father is perfect."* (Matthew 5:48) To preach the gospel without the call to holiness is to lie to God's people by omission. It is to leave them spiritually dead while making them believe they are spiritually alive. And I think we can all agree that this diluted gospel cannot save. It cannot cleanse. And it definitely cannot transform.

As the late Southern Baptist minister Vance Havner once said,

"We are not going to move this world by criticism of it nor conformity to it, but by the combustion within it of lives ignited by the Spirit of God."

To walk in holiness is to burn with God's fire.
It's to carry His fragrance and embody His character.
It's to live in such a way that the world is convicted—not entertained—by our presence.
Holiness is not optional. It is the very evidence that we belong to Christ.

Come Out From Babylon

The tragedy of American Christianity is not merely that it tolerates the world—it has become indistinguishable from it. Churches bear the names of Christ yet echo the voice of culture. Sanctuaries have become platforms for branding. Worship has become a genre. And holiness has become an ancient relic buried beneath layers of modern relevance, compromise and sin-accommodating pastors that are afraid of taking a stance for the gospel and possibly offending someone.

The call to "come out from Babylon" is not a poetic metaphor—it's a divine command.

> *"Come out of her, my people, lest you take part in her sins, lest you share in her plagues."* —**Revelation 18:4 (ESV)**

This is not a call to geographical relocation but to spiritual separation. Babylon represents a system—a seductive power structure built upon pride, luxury, rebellion, and idolatry. It lures the soul with pleasure while simultaneously shackling it with delusion. This is nothing new. Babylon has always been the counterfeit kingdom, a spiritual system of compromise, worldliness, and false religion. It is very much alive and well today—in our entertainment, our culture, our schools, and our churches. That being said, many self-professing believers today are card-carrying Babylonians that claim to have rightful citizenship in Heaven. They sing the songs of Zion on Sunday while drinking the wine of Babylon throughout the rest of their week.

> *"And another angel followed, saying, "Babylon is fallen, is fallen, that great city, because she has made all nations drink of the wine of the wrath of her fornication."* —**Revelation 14:8 NKJV**

It shows up in the entertainment (movies, music, and all forms of media) they consume, the ideologies they embrace, and the sexually perverted lifestyles they protect, defend, and justify —all of these things testify that they have not yet come out from among Babylon. They have merely blended in.

> *"Therefore go out from their midst, and be separate from them, says the Lord, and touch no unclean thing; then I will welcome you."*
> **2 Corinthians 6:17 (ESV)**

You cannot love what God hates and say you love Jesus.
You cannot flirt with darkness and expect to walk in light.
You cannot serve God and Mammon.

> *"No one can serve two masters… You cannot serve both God and money."* —**Matthew 6:24 (NIV)**

But the modern American gospel tells us and the rest of the world that we can. It assures us that we are under grace, even when we are living a life of compromise and spiritual complacency. It paints Jesus as a gentle figure who smiles upon every lifestyle, affirms every identity, and blesses every ambition—as long as we say His name occasionally.

But the real Jesus—the One seated in glory—the Lion of Judah-commands repentance.

He walks among the lampstands with eyes like fire. He rebukes churches. He warns the lukewarm. He speaks of judgment. He demands obedience and holiness.

The Jesus of Scripture is not compatible with the Barney-Jesus of Babylon.

And herein lies the tension: Will the Church come out from Babylon? Will we separate ourselves unto the Lord—not just in ritual, but in reality?

In the book of Daniel, Babylon reappears again, now as a dominating empire that enslaves Israel's best and brightest. Yet even in that foreign land, Daniel, Shadrach, Meshach, and Abednego resolved not to defile themselves. They honored God in exile. They refused to eat Babylon's food or bow to Babylon's idols—even if it meant death.

That's the kind of gospel we need again: one that trains men to boldly live holy lives in the midst of national corruption, not blend in with it.

American Christianity has made peace with Babylon. We've adopted Orwellian newspeak, refusing to call sin by its true name. Thus packaging idolatry as innovation. And shying away from hard truths to retain influence, donors, and seats in pews. But the faithful remnant knows better.

We are not called to be Insta-famous. We are called to be faithful.

Again, to be holy is to be set apart—for God's glory, not our personal gain.

When we preach a gospel that refuses to call people out of Babylon, we preach a powerless message. In effect, the church becomes a toothless lion. A diluted gospel cannot deliver from sin because it refuses to define sin.

Leonard Ravenhill once warned,
"The church used to be a lightning bolt—now it's a cruise ship."

The cruise ship gospel will never survive the storms ahead.
Only those who are anchored in truth will endure.
We must stop asking how close can we get to the line.
We must ask: "How close can I get to Christ?"

The gospel they never preached was a gospel of separation.
Of total devotion.
Of surrender.
Of cleansing.
Of power.
And yes, of cost.

It will cost you comfort, reputation, friends, opportunities, and applause.

But it will gain you Christ.

> *"What accord has Christ with Belial? Or what portion does a believer share with an unbeliever?"* —**2 Corinthians 6:15 (ESV)**

We were never meant to blend in. We were meant to stand out.
And to stand up—unashamed—for the gospel they never preached.

The Goodness of God

When most people think of "the goodness of God," they envision material blessings, comfort, protection, or divine leniency. But Scripture frames God's goodness differently. His goodness is not simply about what He gives—it's about how He leads us to repentance and transforms us into His likeness.

> *"Or do you despise the riches of His goodness, forbearance, and longsuffering, not knowing that the goodness of God leads you to repentance?"* —**Romans 2:4 (NKJV)**

God's goodness is a path—a divine invitation to surrender. It confronts us, calls us out of darkness, and demands a response.

But here is what the gospel they do preach conveniently omits: the same God whose goodness leads to repentance is also the righteous Judge whose patience has a limit.

Holiness is not optional. It is the dividing line between life and death, blessing and curse.

> *"This day I call the heavens and the earth as witnesses against you that I have set before you life and death, blessings and curses. Now choose life, so that you and your children may live."*
> **—Deuteronomy 30:19 (NIV)**

God, in His lovingkindness, gives every believer a choice. But He does not remove the consequences from that choice. The American Church often clings to the parts of God's character that affirm us—grace, love, mercy—while ignoring the parts that confront us—justice, holiness, wrath.

Yet both are part of His goodness.

The same God who spared Nineveh is the One who destroyed Sodom and Gomorrah. The difference? Nineveh repented. Sodom remained stiff-necked.

Even so, God was willing to show mercy if only a handful of righteous people could be found. Abraham's bold intercession reveals just how willing the Lord was to extend His mercy. If only ten righteous people could be found, the cities would be spared (Genesis 18:32). But ten could not be found. And so God's judgment fell.

This is not cruel—it is just. It is holy. It is good.

Deuteronomy 28 lays out in devastating clarity what happens when a people reject the Lord's commandments. The chapter opens with blessings for obedience, but the remainder is a grim chronicle of the curses that unfold when a nation or individual continually chooses rebellion:

> *"Because you did not obey the voice of the Lord your God... you shall be cursed in the city and cursed in the country... The Lord will strike you with wasting disease, with fever and inflammation... The heavens over your head shall be bronze, and the earth under you shall be iron."*
> **—Deuteronomy 28:15, 22–23 (NKJV, abridged)**

This is not a one-time slip. This is the slow descent of a heart hardened over time. It's what happens when God rebuffs and rebukes—and we brush Him off. When He warns—and we ignore Him. When He pleads—and we stiffen our necks.

God is good—but He is not to be mocked.

> *"Do not be deceived: God is not mocked, for whatever one sows, that will he also reap."* **—Galatians 6:7 (ESV)**

This is the side of holiness American Christians often overlook. Holiness isn't just about being close to God—it's about being spared from judgment.

And America will most assuredly face God's judgment if its people will not repent before the Lord who changes not.

We are not exempt because of our prosperity, our past revivals, or our patriotic identity. If we do not turn, we will fall under the same justice that brought Sodom to ruin and caused Israel to be exiled. God is not mocked, and nations are not immune to His righteous judgment. The true gospel doesn't only present God as a forgiving Father—it presents Him as the righteous Judge. His goodness warns before it wounds. His mercy always precedes His wrath. But when His mercy is repeatedly rejected, judgment becomes inevitable.

And the wages of sin is death (Romans 6:23).

That's why God called His people to separate from the surrounding pagan cultures and utterly destroy the idols of the land. Not merely to distance themselves—but to ensure those influences could not return.

"Break down their altars, smash their sacred stones and burn their Asherah poles in the fire; cut down the idols of their gods and wipe out their names from those places." —**Deuteronomy 12:3 (NIV)**

The call was not to tolerate idols. It was to tear them down. Holiness requires radical separation from the unclean, the impure, and the profane. And when Israel failed to obey this call, they fell into the very same idolatry they were warned about. The same pattern is seen in the modern Church when we cozy up to cultural idols like homosexuality and co-existence in the name of relevance or tolerance. We are not called to flirt with the altars of Baal—we are called to demolish them.

Just as Gideon did.

In Judges 6, God called Gideon to tear down his father's altar to Baal and cut down the Asherah pole beside it.

In the darkness of night, Gideon obeyed, fearing the backlash that might result from his actions. And backlash did indeed come. The townspeople were furious and demanded he be put to death. But his father responded with truth and clarity:

"But Joash replied to the hostile crowd around him, 'Are you going to plead Baal's cause? Are you trying to save him? Whoever fights for him shall be put to death by morning! If Baal really is a god, he can defend himself when someone breaks down his altar.'" —**Judges 6:31 (NIV)**

The message still echoes today: Why are we defending the Canaanite idols and perverted practices that the Lord has told us to destroy? Why are we building altars of comfort, celebrity, entertainment, and cultural acceptance? Why are we fighting for Baal when the Lord has called us to fight for Him?

The gospel that is being preached says, "God understands."

The gospel they never preached says, "God understands—but He will judge unrepentant sin. God understands—but His compassion and lovingkindness is not a hall pass for sin or a get-out-of-hell free card. God's holiness demands payment for sin—our sin. This is why Jesus died on the cross—not because He sinned, but because we sinned. Christianity 101. And if we continue to sin, then according to Hebrews 10:26–27, *"If we deliberately keep on sinning after we have received the knowledge of the truth, no sacrifice for sins is left, but only a fearful expectation of judgment and of raging fire that will consume the enemies of God."* This passage highlights the seriousness of persistent, willful sin after accepting Christ and the terrifying consequences that God has promised will follow.

The gospel Jesus preached says,

> *"Repent, for the kingdom of heaven is at hand."*
> **—Matthew 4:17 (KJV)**

The goodness of God is not soft. It is sacred. And it is this very goodness that says:
Return to Me. Be holy as I am holy.
Reject sin. Embrace righteousness.
Choose life. And live.

Transition Paragraph:

The time for comfortable Christianity is over. The true gospel is not a sugar-coated message tailored to suit our preferences—it is a sacred summons to live, walk, and die in holiness. The Lord is calling His people to be holy, to come out from among the world, and to proclaim a gospel that has the power to save. But to do this, we must first rebuild what has been torn down—our altars, our convictions, and our commitment to the Lord. Chapter 6 will take us back to the beginning, to the place where revival begins—not in a crowd, but at an altar. Because before a nation can return to God, and by God I mean the Lord God Almighty, its altars must be rebuilt.

End-of-Chapter Review Questions

1. In what ways has the American church replaced the call to holiness with a more convenient version of the gospel?

_____

_____

2. Why is holiness essential to the Christian life, and what does Scripture say about its necessity?

_____

_____

3. What does it practically look like to "come out from Babylon" in today's society?

_____

_____

4. How can believers identify when they are conforming to the world's values instead of God's truth?

_____

_____

5. Why is it significant that God told His people to utterly destroy pagan altars rather than co-exist with them? How does this apply to your spiritual walk today?

_____

_____

6. In what ways can modern Christianity promote a false sense of security about sin and salvation? How can we guard against embracing a version of faith that lacks true obedience and reverence for God?

_____

_____

7. What idols—personal or cultural—have crept into the American Church, and into your personal relationship with God? What must be done to remove them?

_____

_____

8. How do Deuteronomy 28 and Galatians 6:7 illustrate the consequences of disobedience?

_____

_____

9. Why is God's judgment compatible with His goodness? What biblical examples show both His mercy and His justice?

_____

_____

10. What steps can you personally take to walk in true holiness before the Lord?

_____

_____

Rebuilding the Altar

"Now it came to pass after these things that God tested Abraham, and said to him, 'Abraham!' And he said, 'Here I am.' Then He said, 'Take now your son, your only son Isaac, whom you love, and go to the land of Moriah, and offer him there as a burnt offering on one of the mountains of which I shall tell you.'"
—Genesis 22:1–2 (NKJV)

For every true revival in Scripture, there was an altar. It was never built by accident. It required preparation, intention, and surrender. Altars were places of sacrifice—where something costly was laid down in obedience to God. And they were always the place where God met His people.

In our modern worship services, we've replaced the altar with stages and lights. We offer performances instead of offerings. But until the altar is rebuilt in the hearts of God's people, we will continue to operate with a form of godliness and continue to deny its power (2 Timothy 3:5).

God is calling His people back to the altar. Not a physical one—but the spiritual altar of the heart. The place of obedience. The place of dying to self. The place where fire falls—not on empty noise, but on surrendered lives.

A Study on Abraham

When God told Abraham to sacrifice his son Isaac, it wasn't simply a test of obedience—it was a test of worship. Abraham wasn't asked to raise a banner, lead a service, or recite a declaration. He was asked to lay down what he loved most. And without hesitation, Abraham said yes.

This was not an impulsive act. Abraham rose early the next morning (Genesis 22:3), saddled his donkey, and made the journey to Mount Moriah. He came prepared to worship, and for him, worship meant sacrifice.

What a contrast to modern Christianity.

Today, worship is often equated with singing or the atmosphere of a Sunday service. But in the biblical sense, worship means obedience. It means laying something down. It means saying to God, "You are worth more than this."

Abraham's altar was not just a pile of stones—it was a place where he laid down his future. Isaac was the child of promise. To give him up was to risk the entire legacy God had spoken over Abraham's life. And yet, Abraham believed that even if Isaac died, God would raise him from the dead (Hebrews 11:19).

This is what faith looks like. This is what worship looks like.

> *And Abraham said to his young men, "Stay here with the donkey; the lad and I will go yonder and worship, and we will come back to you."*
> **(Genesis 22:5 NKJV).**

He was already confessing resurrection before he saw deliverance. He knew that God could not lie. If the promise came through Isaac, and God required Isaac, then God must have a way to fulfill His word—even in death.

Altars are built on that kind of faith.

In our lives, Isaac can represent the things we treasure—our dreams, our children, our careers, our ministries, our identity. God isn't asking us to destroy them. He's asking us to surrender them. He's asking, "Will you trust Me with what matters most?"

Many want revival without sacrifice. But there is no fire without wood. There is no glory without death. There is no Pentecost without Calvary.

If we want to rebuild the altar, we must start where Abraham did: with obedience. With trust. With a willingness to lay down everything—even the promises of God—on the altar of surrender.

Only then will the fire fall.

It Don't Take All That

So we must humble ourselves before the Lord and go before Him at the altar—not with excuses, not with defiance, but with brokenness. David cried out,

> "Search me, God, and know my heart; test me and know my anxious thoughts. See if there is any offensive way in me in the way everlasting."
> **(Psalm 139:23–24, NIV).**

That's altar talk and how the process of attaining godly sorrow truly begins. We must plead with the Lord to show us our true condition, to strip away every layer of self-deception and reveal what's really in our hearts. But even then, revelation alone is not enough. We must also plead with Him to grant us godly sorrow—the kind of sorrow that leads to true repentance and lasting transformation.

The prophet Joel declared,

> "Rend your heart and not your garments. Return to the Lord your God, for He is gracious and merciful, slow to anger and abounding in steadfast love" **(Joel 2:13, ESV).**

You see, in ancient Israel, people would tear their clothes in moments of mourning or distress. It was an outward sign of deep grief. But God never wanted performance—He wanted repentance. He wanted heart change.

And without godly sorrow, there is no true heart change.

Without godly sorrow, we simply go through the motions. We might show up to church, raise our hands, cry a few tears—but deep down, we remain unbroken. We cling to our sin with a death grip while pretending to worship with open hands.

Godly sorrow cannot be manufactured. It is not the same as guilt or regret. It is a divine gift—a holy heaviness that comes when the Spirit of God convicts us of sin and awakens us to the weight of our offense against a holy God. And where do we receive this gift? At the altar.

When you rebuild the altar of the Lord in your heart and your home, godly sorrow is one of the first offerings He gives in return. It's not glamorous. It is profoundly painful. But it is also powerful. It is freedom. It is the key that unlocks every chained door in your soul.

James lays out this exact process in unmistakable clarity:

> *"Draw near to God, and He will draw near to you. Cleanse your hands, you sinners; and purify your hearts, you double-minded. Be afflicted, and mourn, and weep. Let your laughter be turned to mourning and your joy to heaviness. Humble yourselves in the sight of the Lord, and He shall lift you up."* — **James 4:8–10, KJV**

This is what godly sorrow looks like: mourning over sin, feeling its weight, and turning from it. When the Lord reveals the truth about your sin and where you really stand before Him, it will shatter you. Your laughing will immediately be turned to mourning. Your joy turned into heaviness. But the process doesn't end there—it ends in resurrection, renovation, and restoration. When we humble ourselves before God, He doesn't crush us—He lifts us. He raises us up from the ashes, cleansed and made whole. The very sorrow that brought us low becomes the soil from which revival grows.

Godly sorrow will help you walk in the liberty that you've read about but never fully experienced. It will empower you to live in the promises of Scripture—not just as ideals, but as daily reality. It will close every hidden back door that the enemy has used to re-enter your life.

This—this is how you walk in victory. This is how you become a man or woman who fears the Lord and obeys His commandments. And this is the person in whom the Lord delights. Not the most eloquent. Not the most famous. The most surrendered.

That being said, among many believers—especially in the African-American church—there's a familiar phrase often uttered with a knowing nod: "It don't take all that." It's shorthand for a more complete thought: "It doesn't take all of that to serve God." In essence, it's a way of saying that the sacrifices someone else is making for the Lord are excessive or unnecessary. But every time I hear this, I can't help but wonder—what Bible are they reading??

Because my Bible says something entirely different.

Peter wrote,

> *"If the righteous one is scarcely saved, where will the ungodly and the sinner appear?"* **(1 Peter 4:18, NKJV).**

That word "scarcely" means with great difficulty. Not ease. Not convenience. Not casual effort. Difficulty.

When we describe something as "difficult," we understand it's hard to do. It takes effort. It's not for the faint of heart. Being fluent in Mandarin is difficult. Understanding quantum physics is difficult. Likewise, the Bible tells us that salvation itself—for the righteous—is difficult.

Let that sink in: If it is difficult for the righteous to be saved, what does that say about the modern, half-hearted approach we often see in American Christianity? If all it took was saying a prayer, attending a church service, and reading a Bible verse here and there, would God really call that "difficult"? Of course not. That's easy. And that's exactly the problem.

When God calls you to put to death something you love on His altar because of its satanic origins—Christmas, Easter, Halloween—many balk. "Wait now, Lord. I grew up celebrating these. I love these traditions. They're part of who I am. Everybody else is celebrating those holidays; it's just good clean fun!" Now see...that sounds difficult. But consider this: Anton LaVey, the founder of the church of Satan, himself declared that by dressing up, either by wearing a costume or by coloring oneself in celebration of Halloween, signifies that you allow Satan to own you. He further said that when you adopt the pagan practices, you subconsciously dedicate yourself to the devil. He took joy in Christians who take part in the tradition, saying:

I am glad that Christian parents let their children worship the devil at least one night out of the year. Welcome to Halloween. - Anton LaVey, Founder of the Church of Satan

How about when He asks you to stop watching the movies and tv shows you adore—Star Wars, Game of Thrones, Harry Potter, or Pokémon—because they open spiritual doors you didn't even realize were there? "But Lord, there's nothing wrong with it. it's just a movie, it's just a tv show, it's just a game!" Now see...that sounds difficult.

Or maybe He puts His finger on your sexual desires. "What do you mean I have to give up pornography? What do you mean same-sex relationships are sinful and I'm not allowed to serve in the ministry at church? But Lord, I love this… I feel like I was born this way!" Now see...that sounds difficult.

Or maybe the Holy Spirit calls you to let go of worldly pop, rap and R&B music because witches cast spells on the master recordings which open you up to demonic activity every time you play it. "Wait a minute Lord. You're going too far now. You don't really expect me to listen to church music for the rest of my life?!" And yes. That sounds difficult.

Actually, that sounds like sacrifice. And that's exactly the point.

But then again, if being saved were easy—if it didn't take "all that"—why would Jesus say the road to life is narrow and only a few find it?

The truth is, many people simply don't want to do what's really required. They don't want to let go of their idols. So, like the rich young ruler, they walk away sad —not because Jesus turned them away, but because He asked for what they treasured most, what they loved the most, and they weren't willing to lay it down.

We are quick to read those stories in Scripture and nod in agreement. But when it's our turn—when God puts our Isaacs on the altar—we are quick to pump the brakes. And as the saying goes, 'slow obedience is no obedience.' Now let's be clear about something here: Abraham didn't just love Isaac. He adored him. He waited decades for him.

But when God said "offer him," Abraham quickly obeyed. Again, slow obedience is no obedience.

So what about you? What are you holding onto that God is telling you to sacrifice?

Maybe it's your relationship, your identity, your shows, your (pick whatever sin of your choosing). Whatever it is, the altar is still the place where all idols die and all holiness begins.

If you're not walking in freedom, it's not because God failed—it's because you've allowed a back door open to the enemy. You've tolerated things the Lord never intended for you to carry. You've called sin by another name, excused it, coddled it, defended and protected it, even justified it. You may even say, like I did about placing Star Wars and Game of Thrones/House of Dragons on His altar, "But Lord I love this thing!"

And His response: "Do you love it more than Me?"

That's the real question.

And you need to be honest with yourself; the Lord already knows the truth. But here's the beauty of the altar—it's not just a place of death. It's also a place of transformation. The moment you confess, "Lord, I do love this sin—but I love You more," and lay it down before Him, that's when deliverance begins.

That's how idols get torn down. That's how godly legacies are built.

Because yes—it does take all that.

But wait! There's more good news: God will honor your sacrifice. 1 Samuel 2:30 tells us that God will honor those that honor Him. Every offering laid down on the altar doesn't just cost you—it draws you closer to Him. He responds not only with cleansing, but with transformation. He gives you new desires—godly desires. He begins to shape your heart into a mirror of His own.

The things that move God will begin to move you.
The things that grieve His Spirit will start to grieve yours.
What once made you laugh now brings you to tears.
What once seemed harmless now stirs holy anger.
What once delighted your flesh now feels foreign to your soul.

Because when you surrender, God doesn't just remove sin—*He replaces it with Himself.* His Spirit fills the empty spaces, His love rewrites your affections, and His holiness becomes your hunger.

This is not legalism.
This is not extremism.
This is transformation.
This is what it means to be alive in Christ and dead to sin.

So yes—it does take all that.

And everything you give up for God, He returns with something far greater: more of Himself.

Walking in the Light

The proof of our repentance is not in what we say—it's in how we live.

> *"If we claim to have fellowship with Him and yet walk in darkness, we lie and do not live out the truth. But if we walk in the light, as He is in the light, we have fellowship with one another, and the blood of Jesus, His Son, purifies us from all sin."* —**1 John 1:6–7 (NIV)**

To walk in the light is not merely about avoiding darkness—it is about living in alignment with the truth of God's Word. It is about integrity. Consistency. Full exposure to the holy light of God that reveals, heals, and purifies.

Far too many believers live double lives—Sunday saints and weekday wanderers. We lift our hands in worship while keeping hidden compartments in our hearts. We quote Scripture but compromise in secret. And yet we still believe we are "covered."

But light and darkness cannot coexist.

> *"This is the message we have heard from him and declare to you: God is light; in Him there is no darkness at all."* —**1 John 1:5 (NIV)**

The altar you rebuild must be lit by truth, not pretense. You can't rebuild it with unconfessed sin or hidden idols. You can't approach God as though He cannot see. He sees it all. He knows the secret things. He knows the justifications we've rehearsed for years. But He also knows what's possible if we will simply come into the light.

Too many of us confuse spiritual activity with spiritual vitality. Just because you're busy for God doesn't mean you're walking with God. There's no substitute for intimacy, no program that replaces repentance, and no performance that impresses the Holy One of Israel.

The light doesn't just expose—it heals.

Jesus said, "Everyone who does evil hates the light, and will not come into the light for fear that their deeds will be exposed. But whoever lives by the truth comes into the light, so that it may be seen plainly that what they have done has been done in the sight of God." (John 3:20–21, NIV). When we walk in the light, shame loses its grip. Deception dies. Healing begins. And the altar becomes a place of transformation, not condemnation.

This is the path of the faithful.
This is the journey of the holy.
And this is what it means to rebuild the altar.

Arise and Shine

> *"Arise, shine; for your light has come! And the glory of the Lord is risen upon you."* —**Isaiah 60:1 (NKJV)**

Once we've rebuilt the altar of the Lord, we don't stay lying prostrate on the floor forever. At some point, we must rise. The altar is where we die—but it's also where we are resurrected. It is where we are broken—but also where we are made whole. After the fire of repentance comes the glory of revival.

To arise is to take your place in the army of God. To shine is to reflect His glory in a darkened world.

This is not a call to be a celebrity—it's a call to be consecrated.
The Lord is looking for those who will carry His presence with purity, who will speak with boldness, and who will love without compromise. The altar isn't a hiding place. It's a launching pad. Let's look at God's process for revival.

Elijah rebuilt the altar, called upon the Lord and then fire fell from heaven. The early Church prayed—and the Spirit was poured out with power. Jesus submitted to the Father—even to death—and then rose in glory.

So what are you waiting for??

For crying out loud! The American Church doesn't need any more events. It needs more obedient believers who have touched the altar and carry the flame. Our culture doesn't need more opinions. It needs more godly witnesses—those who arise from the ashes with the fragrance of Christ.

But you cannot shine until you've been lit.
You cannot arise until you've first died to self.
You cannot carry the weight of glory unless you've stood under the weight of Holy Spirit conviction.

The enemy has tried to lull the Church to sleep with comfort, distraction, and compromise. But the trumpet is sounding. The Bridegroom is coming. And the call is clear:

> *"Wake up, sleeper, rise from the dead, and Christ will shine on you."*
> **—Ephesians 5:14 (NIV)**

You were not made to blend in. You were not called to survive. You were appointed to arise and shine—to boldly bear the light of Christ in a world gone dim.

The altar is not just a place of surrender. It is the starting point of divine assignment. It is the birthplace of movements, the cradle of miracles, the fuel for fearless living. And this is really what moved me to write this book.

Over the course of two years, the Holy Spirit has been convicting me to rebuild the altar in my heart. Step by step I built it. Sacrifice by sacrifice I built it. I recently watched a Pastor John Mulinde sermon on Nick Jones' YouTube channel where the Lord told him if He came back now, He wouldn't be taking Pastor John with him because of his thought life.

Here's the link for the video:
https://youtu.be/3Z-DUgJicYY?si=6IWdSWbucV5Ss0RQ

I was terrified and immediately went before the altar of the Lord to lay down my entire life for Him...again. After arising from the altar, the word that was reverberating in my spirit was: **_holiness._** I couldn't stop hearing Hebrews 12:14 in my heart:

Pursue peace with all people, and holiness, without which no one will see the Lord.

I determined to write this book and get the word out to the Body of Christ. Immediately.
The time for passivity is over.
The time for compromise is over.
The time for holiness is <u>now</u>.

Rebuild the altar in your heart and in your home. Allow the Lord to make you a flame of fire. Arise and shine.

Abide in His Word

> *"Then Jesus said to those Jews who believed Him, 'If you abide in My word, you are My disciples indeed. And you shall know the truth, and the truth shall make you free.'"* **—John 8:31–32 (NKJV)**

The fire on the altar was never meant to be a one-time blaze—it was meant to be kept burning continuously (Leviticus 6:13). And the way we keep that fire alive is by abiding in the Word of God.

To abide means to dwell, remain, continue. It is more than a morning devotional. It is more than a Sunday sermon. It is a daily posture of obedience and intimacy with the voice of the Lord through Scripture.

The American Church has traded depth for convenience. We highlight verses without heeding them. We memorize Scripture without meditating on it. We quote it without living it. But Jesus made it clear—only those who abide in His Word are His disciples.

You can't be a disciple if you only visit the Word occasionally.
You won't be transformed by truth if you're still living off motivational quotes and half-context sermons.

The Word of God is not optional. It is oxygen. It is the bread of life (John 6:35), the sword of the Spirit (Ephesians 6:17), a lamp to our feet and a light to our path (Psalm 119:105). And in this hour of deception and delusion, we must return to it with holy reverence.

If the altar is where we surrender, and the fire is where we're refined, then the Word is where we are anchored. The storms will come. The winds will howl. But the one who builds their house on the rock of God's Word will never be moved (Matthew 7:24–27).

To rebuild the altar in your life is to return to His Word and commit yourself to obeying it...no matter what.

Not just to study it. Not just to teach it. Not just to quote it.
But to be fully submitted to it. To live by it. To be ruled by it.
Because Jesus is the Word made flesh. You cannot separate your relationship with Him from your relationship with the Scriptures.

You may sing, you may pray, you may serve—but if you do not abide in His Word, you are vulnerable to deception, to burnout, to drift.

Many believers wonder why they don't hear God speak—but their Bibles remain closed. God has already spoken in His Word. The question is: Have we listened?

Revival does not come through emotions. It comes through our submission and alignment with the Lord. And nothing aligns us with God's heart like His Word.

In a generation filled with noise, confusion, and shifting truths, there must rise a people who stand on the unshakable, unchangeable, everlasting Word of the living God.

Rebuild the altar.

Let the fire fall.

Then abide in His Word—daily, deeply, and without compromise.

This is how we overcome.

This is how we walk in power until the very end.

Aloha My Dear Brother or Sister in Christ

If you've made it this far, then you've felt the weight of truth pressing against your spirit. This book was never meant to entertain or tickle ears — it was meant to awaken, confront, and call forth God's holy remnant in the midst of a crooked generation. It was written for the one who knows deep down that something is very wrong — not just with the world, but with much of what we've accepted as "church."

We are a people living in perilous times. The lines between righteousness and rebellion have been blurred by compromise, convenience, and cultural Christianity. Many are sleepwalking through faith, clinging to cultural traditions, and what they personally feel or think will get them into Heaven, but are void of the power and presence of the Living God.

But there is a remnant rising. A remnant who will not allow themselves to be labeled or defined by anything other than the Word of God.

A remnant who believe every jot and tittle of the Word of God and are committed to obeying it.

A people who are not content with powerless religion.
A people who still tremble at His Word.
A people who deeply desire the fire of the Holy Spirit in their lives and won't settle for anything less.

Let this be your invitation to step fully into the narrow way. *Rebuild the altar. Tear down every idol. Lay down every weight and sin that so easily entangles.* You are not called to blend in — **you are called to burn brightly.**

> *"He makes His angels spirits, And His servants a flame of fire."*
> **— Hebrews 1:7 (NKJV)**

> *"Arise, shine; For your light has come! And the glory of the Lord is risen upon you."* **— Isaiah 60:1 NKJV**

This is your calling: to burn with holy fire. To shine with uncompromising truth. To arise and be the light in a world that has lost its way.

The days ahead will be dark. But the light of Christ shines brightest in the midnight hour.

This is the hour of separation.
This is the hour of consecration.
This is the hour of repentance.
This is the hour of return.

If we would humble ourselves and return to the Lord with weeping, fasting, and brokenness, He has promised to heal. To revive. To restore. You may feel unworthy. You may feel unequipped.

But God never asked for your resume — He asked for your heart.

So give Him your heart.
Give Him your yes.
Give Him your all.

Not tomorrow. Not someday. **Now.**

> *"And do this, understanding the present time: The hour has already come for you to wake up from your slumber, because our salvation is nearer now than when we first believed."* **—Romans 13:11 (NIV)**

"Do you not say, 'There are still four months and then comes the harvest'? Behold, I say to you, lift up your eyes and look at the fields, for they are already white for harvest!" **—John 4:35 NKJV**

The fields are white for harvest. The Bridegroom is at the door. May He find you ready.

—Michael M. Dillard

Verse by Verse Breakdown

Verse 30

"Then Elijah said to all the people, 'Come near to me.' So all the people came near to him. And he repaired the altar of the Lord that was broken down."

Insight: Revival begins with a return to true worship. Elijah doesn't start with performance—he starts by repairing what had been neglected. The altar is symbolic of the heart of Israel's covenant with God. Like many believers today, the altar had been broken down and forgotten.

Verse 31

"And Elijah took twelve stones, according to the number of the tribes of the sons of Jacob, to whom the word of the Lord had come, saying, 'Israel shall be your name.'"

Insight: Elijah doesn't forget who they are. Even in apostasy, Israel's identity is still rooted in the covenant. The twelve stones remind the people of their unity and their calling. True repentance calls us back to who we really are in God.

Verse 32

"Then with the stones he built an altar in the name of the Lord; and he made a trench around the altar large enough to hold two seahs of seed."

Insight: The altar is rebuilt with reverence and intentionality. The trench signifies preparation for overflow and sacrifice. Elijah is making room—not just for the fire—but for the evidence of God's glory.

Verse 33

"And he put the wood in order, cut the bull in pieces, and laid it on the wood, and said, 'Fill four waterpots with water, and pour it on the burnt sacrifice and on the wood.'"

Insight: Elijah doesn't make it easier for God to show up—he makes it harder. Drenching the sacrifice proves this is no trick. Revival isn't about hype; it's about God making Himself known in unmistakable power.

Verse 34

"Then he said, 'Do it a second time,' and they did it a second time; and he said, 'Do it a third time,' and they did it a third time."

Insight: The repetition emphasizes obedience and faith. Elijah is boldly confident that God will respond—not despite the water, but through it. Sometimes God waits until all natural hope is gone before He moves.

Verse 35

"So the water ran all around the altar; and he also filled the trench with water."

Insight: Every part of the altar is soaked. No corner is left untouched. Likewise, full surrender means allowing the Spirit to saturate every area of our lives—nothing withheld.

Verse 36

"And it came to pass, at the time of the offering of the evening sacrifice, that Elijah the prophet came near and said, 'Lord God of Abraham, Isaac, and Israel, let it be known this day that You are God in Israel and I am Your servant, and that I have done all these things at Your word.'"

Insight: Elijah's prayer is short, direct, and powerful. His motive isn't personal glory—it's that the people would know that **God is God**, and that everything he has done was in obedience.

Verse 37

"Hear me, O Lord, hear me, that this people may know that You are the Lord God, and that You have turned their hearts back to You again."

Insight: This is the goal of revival—not just signs and wonders, but hearts turning back to God. Elijah understands the true work of the Spirit is inward, not just external. His cry is for national repentance and restoration.

Verse 38

"Then the fire of the Lord fell and consumed the burnt sacrifice, and the wood and the stones and the dust, and it licked up the water that was in the trench."

Insight: God answers with fire! Every element—sacrifice, altar, dust, water—is consumed. This is total affirmation from heaven. The fire represents God's holy presence, His acceptance, and His purifying power.

Verse 39

"Now when all the people saw it, they fell on their faces; and they said, 'The Lord, He is God! The Lord, He is God!'"

Insight: The people finally respond in unified repentance and worship. Fire brought them to their knees—not because of fear alone, but awe. **This is the fruit of revival.** Broken altars rebuilt, God answering by fire, and the people returning to Him.

Devotional: 30 Days of Repentence, Renewal, and Fire

30-Day Devotional Plan
Table of Contents

Rebuild the Altar

Scripture Focus:

"Then Elijah said to all the people, 'Come near to me.' So all the people came near to him. And he repaired the altar of the Lord that was broken down." — **1 Kings 18:30 (NKJV)**

Devotional Thought:

The first step toward revival is repairing the altar. In Elijah's day, the altar had been broken and neglected—symbolizing Israel's forsaking of their covenant relationship with God. For us today, the "altar" represents our hearts, our homes, and our daily lives where God is meant to reign.

Is your altar broken?

Sometimes we go through the motions of religion while our altar lies in ruins—prayer has become mechanical, repentance is shallow, and compromise seeps in. But Elijah didn't start with fire. He started with repair. Before the heavens answered, the altar had to be restored.

Rebuilding the altar is a deliberate act. Elijah gathered stones—one for each tribe—reminding Israel of their identity and calling. You, too, are chosen and called. Today is the day to remember who you are and return to your first love.

And don't be discouraged by the condition of the altar. It's never too broken for God to restore. The moment you say "yes" to rebuilding, God leans in.

Prayer:

Father, thank You for Your amazing love and mercy. Please show me all of the places in my heart where the altar has been broken down. I am guilty of turning my back to you, neglecting my First Love and compromising my walk before You. Please forgive me! Please help me to rebuild what I have broken and neglected. Please create in me a clean heart and renew within me a right spirit that honors and seeks You first. May You begin revival in me—starting today. In Jesus' name! Amen.

Reflection Questions:

What part of your spiritual life needs repair or attention today?

_____

_____

Have you allowed compromise to erode the altar of your heart?

_____

_____

Are you willing to begin again, even if it requires effort, humility, and honesty?

_____

_____

Action Step:

Set aside 15 quiet minutes today to pray and begin listing areas where you've strayed from full surrender. Invite God to reveal where the altar needs to be rebuilt. Write down what He shows you.

Draw Near to God

Scripture:

> *"Draw near to God and He will draw near to you. Cleanse your hands, you sinners; and purify your hearts, you double-minded. Lament and mourn and weep! Let your laughter be turned to mourning and your joy to gloom. Humble yourselves in the sight of the Lord, and He will lift you up."* —**James 4:8–10 (NKJV)**

Devotional

It's one thing to know that something is wrong. It's another to weep over it. God isn't just calling us to be aware of our sin—He's calling us to feel it the way He does. To lament over our rebellion. To mourn our compromise. To weep over the ways we've dishonored Him.

James 4 doesn't soften the message—it intensifies it: Cleanse your hands. Purify your hearts. Stop pretending everything is fine while secretly holding onto compromise. It's time to trade worldly laughter for holy mourning. That's what godly sorrow does—it brings a brokenness that leads to wholeness.

But here's the promise: if you draw near to God, He will draw near to you. He's not hiding. He's waiting.

This isn't condemnation—it's invitation. The heart that humbles itself will be lifted up by God Himself. You don't have to fix yourself. You just have to get honest and step closer to Him. The altar is open.

Prayer

Father, thank You for being so kind and merciful to me a sinful person. May You have mercy on my soul. Please help me to clean my hands and purify my heart as I don't know how to do this on my own. Please forgive me for being double-minded, for I know You said that a double-minded man should expect nothing from You. Please lead me to godly sorrow, remove my heart of stone and give me a heart of flesh. I choose You Father. No matter what I choose You. I love You and thank You in Jesus' name! Amen.

Reflection Questions

What area of your life have you been hiding or excusing instead of surrendering?

_____

_____

Have you experienced true godly sorrow before? What did it produce in you?

_____

_____

In what ways do you need to humble yourself today?

_____

_____

Repent and Return

Scripture:

"'Now, therefore,' says the Lord, 'Turn to Me with all your heart, with fasting, with weeping, and with mourning.' So rend your heart, and not your garments; return to the Lord your God, for He is gracious and merciful, slow to anger, and of great kindness; and He relents from doing harm." —**Joel 2:12–13 (NKJV)**

Devotional

God doesn't want your performance—He wants your heart.

In ancient Israel, people would often tear their clothes to show outward grief, but God was never impressed by outward displays. What He really desired was inward brokenness. The kind of sorrow that tears the heart, not just the shirt.

Joel's prophetic word is as urgent today as it was then: Turn to the Lord with all your heart. With fasting. With weeping. With mourning. In other words, let your repentance cost you something. Let it be full-bodied and real—not performative or shallow.

And why should we return to Him? Because He is gracious, merciful, slow to anger, and abundantly kind. He doesn't delight in judgment. He delights in mercy. But mercy flows toward the humble and the broken.

When we return to God in sincerity, we don't just escape consequences—we encounter His heart. That's what revival is. Not just avoiding harm, but being restored to the One who loves us enough to call us back.

Prayer

Father, thank You for Your unfailing love and all the many ways that You show me, a sinful person, Your great love every day. I have allowed myself to drift from You and I've allowed my heart to grow cold before You. Please forgive me! Please grant me godly sorrow that leads to repentance! Please help me to rend my heart, oh Lord. May You have mercy on me because You love me and You desire to do so. I ask these things in the name of Jesus! Amen.

Reflection Questions

What outward behaviors have you used to cover an inward struggle?

_____

_____

What does it look like for you to truly "rend your heart" before the Lord?

_____

_____

How has God shown His mercy to you in the past when you repented?

_____

_____

Rebuild the Altar

Scripture:

"Then Elijah said to all the people, 'Come near to me.' So all the people came near to him. And he repaired the altar of the Lord that was broken down." —**1 Kings 18:30 (NKJV)**

Devotional

Before God sent His fire from heaven, Elijah did something vital—he repaired the altar. The altar had been torn down by neglect, compromise, and idolatry. It was no longer a place of consecration, but a forgotten relic.

Sound familiar?

Many of us have allowed the altar of the Lord in our lives—our prayer life, our devotion, our holiness—to fall into disrepair. We've let busyness, sin, or cultural compromise dismantle the place where fire once fell. And now we wonder why the fire is missing.

Before revival comes, rebuilding must come. The altar is symbolic of surrender, repentance, and worship. When you rebuild it—whether through fasting, prayer, repentance, or removing idols from your home and heart—you prepare a place for the presence and power of God.

Elijah didn't just call on God. He made a place where God would be welcomed. That's your call today. Rebuild what has been broken. Return what has been stolen. Repent for what's been tolerated.

And then... watch for the fire.

Prayer

Father, blessed be Your great and holy name! Thank You for allowing me to be the apple of Your eye at all times. May You have mercy on my soul and lead me in Your paths. I have lost my way and need Your help and lovingkindness. Please forgive me for leaning unto my own understanding! Please show me how to rebuild the altar of the Lord according to Your specifications for You are the Great and Holy Builder of all creation. Thank you so much. In Jesus' name. Amen.

Reflection Questions

What areas of your spiritual life have been neglected or broken down?

_____

_____

What does "rebuilding the altar" practically look like in your life this week?

_____

_____

Are there any idols that need to be removed before God's fire can fall?

_____

_____

God Answers by Fire

Scripture:

"Then the fire of the Lord fell and consumed the burnt sacrifice, and the wood and the stones and the dust, and it licked up the water that was in the trench. Now when all the people saw it, they fell on their faces; and they said, 'The Lord, He is God! The Lord, He is God!'"
— 1 Kings 18:38–39 (NKJV)

Devotional

When Elijah rebuilt the altar and laid the sacrifice in obedience, he prayed only once—and heaven responded with fire. Not thunder. Not a gentle breeze. But fire—a consuming, undeniable, supernatural display of God's presence and power.

Why fire?

Because fire purifies, it consumes, it confirms. Fire is God's signature upon sacrifice. It's His way of saying, "I received this offering. I accept this surrender."

But there's a pattern to God's fire: first comes obedience, then the sacrifice, and then the fire.

Too many people cry out for God to send revival fire while refusing to place anything on the altar. No brokenness. No repentance. No real sacrifice. Yet Elijah's fire didn't fall until the wood, the bull, the stones, and even the water were laid before the Lord.

Today, if you want God to respond by fire in your life, ask yourself: Have I truly laid it all down?

When the people saw the fire fall, they knew—The Lord, He is God! The fire didn't just confirm Elijah's ministry—it convicted the people's hearts.

Prayer

Father, may Your holy name be honored in my life. Thank You for Your goodness and Your everlasting faithfulness. I am guilty of doubting You and looking to other things and people to meet my needs. Please forgive me for my double-mindedness and adultery before You. Please help me to love the Lord my God with all my heart, all my soul, and all my strength that I may find You. I love You and I desperately need You to survive in this world. Thank You for hearing my petition and answering with a yes and amen. I ask these things in the holy name of Jesus. Amen.

Reflection Questions

What part of your life needs to be laid on the altar today?

_____

_____

Are you expecting God's fire without first offering full surrender?

_____

_____

When God's fire falls, how will you respond?

_____

_____

DAY 6

Obedience Precedes Power

Scripture:

"And Elijah said to all the people, 'Come near to me.' So all the people came near to him. And he repaired the altar of the Lord that was broken down." —**1 Kings 18:30 (NKJV)**

Devotional

Before the fire fell from heaven… before the people repented… before revival swept the land—Elijah rebuilt the altar.

He didn't start with a loud prayer. He didn't start with fire. He started with obedience.

One of the most overlooked truths in the Christian life is this: power always follows obedience.

We often want God to move in power without yielding in obedience. But God's presence does not rest upon the disobedient. Even Jesus said, *"If you love Me, keep My commandments"* (John 14:15). Elijah didn't call down fire until he first repaired what was broken.

In many of our lives, God's power is withheld not because He is unwilling, but because we are unyielding. The altar of prayer has been neglected. The altar of repentance has been dismantled. The altar of worship has been overgrown with weeds of worldliness.

Before we see fire fall, we must repair the altar.

Obedience is the wood. Sacrifice is the offering. And the altar is the place where heaven meets earth.

Prayer

Father, thank You for your great love. For who is like You in all the earth and whom do I have in heaven besides You? I have been disobedient and have gone astray from Your holy teachings. I have walked in the ways of my flesh. Please forgive me for this Father and teach me Your will that I may obey You in all things. Thank You for loving me so much. I love You. In Jesus' wonderful name. Amen.

Reflection Questions

What "altar" in your life needs to be rebuilt?

_____

_____

Have you delayed obedience in any area God has already spoken about?

_____

_____

How have you seen God move after obedience in your past?

_____

_____

Repairing the Altar of the Heart

Scripture:

Then Elijah called to the people, "Come over here!" They all crowded around him as he repaired the altar of the Lord that had been torn down. He took twelve stones, one to represent each of the tribes of Israel,
—1 Kings 18:30–31 (NLT)

Devotional

When Elijah rebuilt the altar, he didn't build it haphazardly. He used twelve stones, each one representing the tribes of Israel, the covenant people of God. He was intentional. Deliberate. Reverent.

Likewise, the Lord is calling us to repair the altar of the heart—not carelessly, but carefully. Piece by piece. Stone by stone.

Some of us have hearts scattered by disappointment, shattered by compromise, or hardened by sin. But God never discards broken altars— He restores them. The restoration begins with honesty, followed by repentance, and completed through yielded surrender.

Elijah rebuilt the altar using what God had already ordained: stones of identity and covenant. In the same way, God calls us to rebuild using truth, faith, and grace—stones He has already placed in our spiritual inheritance.

When we allow God to rebuild the altar of our hearts, we become candidates for fire. Revival doesn't fall on rebellion—it falls on consecration.

Prayer

Father, thank You for loving me and always instructing me in the way I should go. I have not trusted in the Lord my God to build my life. But rather I leaned unto my own understanding. Father, please forgive me for sinning against You. Please show me Your will for my life. Please grant me the ears to hear what thus sayeth the Lord! Thank you Father. In Jesus' name. Amen.

Reflection Questions

What specific areas of your heart need to be rebuilt or surrendered today?

_____

_____

Are you building with God's materials—His truth, grace, and covenant promises?

_____

_____

How can you daily offer your heart as a holy altar to the Lord?

_____

_____

When Fire Falls

Scripture:

"Then the fire of the Lord fell and consumed the burnt sacrifice, and the wood and the stones and the dust, and it licked up the water that was in the trench." —**1 Kings 18:38 (NKJV)**

Devotional

The altar was rebuilt. The offering was prepared. The prayer was lifted. And then—it happened. Fire fell.

When God responds with fire, it's never subtle. It consumes everything. Not just the sacrifice, but the wood, the stones, the dust, and even the water in the trench. This wasn't a flicker—it was a declaration from heaven.

What made the fire fall? Not just Elijah's prayer, but the obedience, preparation, and surrender that preceded it. The altar had been restored. The people's hearts were ready. The prophet stood in alignment with God's will.

In our own lives, we often want fire without sacrifice, revival without repentance, power without purity. But the fire of the Lord falls where there is surrender. It falls where hearts have been emptied of pride, sin, and self.

God's fire brings clarity. It reveals what is holy and what is not. It burns away falsehood and fuels transformation.

Today, prepare your altar. Offer your life. And stand back—because when fire falls, everything changes.

Prayer

Father, thank You for being the Judge of all the earth. Thank You for Your kindness and Your great mercy! I have loved the world and its ungodly ways. Please forgive me Father! I lay my entire life down before You right now! All that I have or ever will have, all that I am or ever will be I lay down before You now. I lay down all my dreams, rights, possessions, and every relationship before You right now. I consider them all as garbage for the sake of knowing You and loving You! Please search my heart and burn away any and every thing that is not of You and does not please You. I love You so much Father! Thank You so much! In Jesus' mighty name. Amen.

Reflection Questions

Have you fully prepared your altar—your life—for God's fire?

_____

_____

What might God be asking you to lay down so His presence can fully consume you?

_____

_____

Are you ready for the kind of change that God's fire brings?

_____

_____

You Are the Temple

Scripture:

"Do you not know that you are the temple of God and that the Spirit of God dwells in you?" —**1 Corinthians 3:16 (NKJV)**

Devotional

In the Old Testament, God's presence dwelled in tabernacles and temples—holy spaces constructed according to His specifications. But under the New Covenant, the dwelling place of God has shifted. He no longer lives in buildings made by human hands. He lives in you.

You are the temple. Not your church, not a revival tent, not even a mountain-top prayer room. You.

That truth changes everything. The temple had to be kept holy, purified, and consecrated. And so must you. This isn't legalism—it's honor. You are carrying the presence of the Most High God. Every word you speak, every thought you entertain, every action you take—God is present.

When Jesus overturned the money changers' tables in the temple courts, it was because the sacred had been profaned. The same warning applies today. When we fill our lives with compromise, idolatry, or impurity, we grieve the Spirit who lives within us.

But the good news? As the temple, you're not just a passive structure. You are a living house of worship, filled with purpose and power. So cleanse the temple. Welcome His presence. And carry His glory with reverence and joy.

Prayer

Lord, thank You for your unfailing love and grace. Thank You for choosing me to serve You before the beginning of the world. You saw me and all my many sins and You still chose to love me anyway. Oh God...I have failed to remember that my body is Your temple. Please forgive me and teach me how to take care of this temple of Yours. Please help me to do this because I cannot do it in my own strength. I love You Father. Thank you. In Jesus' precious name. Amen.

Reflection Questions

In what ways might you have forgotten that your body is the temple of the Holy Spirit?

_____

_____

What habits, attitudes, or influences need to be removed to make more room for God's presence?

_____

_____

How can you actively honor God's Spirit dwelling within you today?

_____

_____

Restore the Altar in Your Home

Scripture:

"Then Elijah said to all the people, 'Come near to me.' So all the people came near to him. And he repaired the altar of the Lord that was broken down." —**1 Kings 18:30 (NKJV)**

Devotional

Before the fire of God fell on Mount Carmel, before the supernatural display of heaven's power silenced the prophets of Baal, Elijah did something seemingly simple—he repaired the altar.

The altar had been neglected, torn down, forgotten. Sound familiar?

Many households today reflect the same condition. Prayer is sporadic. The Word is rarely opened. The name of God is known, but His presence isn't welcomed. The altar is in disrepair.

But here's the key: revival doesn't begin in the church building—it begins in your living room. In your kitchen. Around your dinner table. At the foot of your bed. You don't need a pulpit to encounter God. You need an altar—a place of sacrifice, devotion, and communion.

Elijah rebuilt the altar with twelve stones—one for each tribe of Israel— reminding the people of their covenant with God. What might your "stones" look like? Time in the Word. Corporate family prayer. Fasting together. Repentance. Gratitude. Worship.

When the altar is rebuilt, God responds with fire.

Prayer

Father, thank You for being the Almighty God of Israel. Your power has never diminished and Your kingdom is an everlasting kingdom. May You please forgive me for the many ways I have taken Your great name in vain. Please forgive me for the many ways that I have been lukewarm. May You not spit me out of Your mouth! Oh God, please give me a heart of flesh, please give me Your heart so that I am moved by the things that move You. Please remove this heart of stone from me. I cannot do this on my own. If You don't help me, then I won't be helped. Have mercy on me! I love You! Thank You in Jesus' name! Amen.

Reflection Questions

Is there a designated time or space in your home where God is regularly honored?

_____

_____

What can you do this week to restore or create a family altar?

_____

_____

What distractions might you need to remove to give God first place in your household?

_____

_____

Repentance Is the Reset Button

Scripture:

"Repent therefore and be converted, that your sins may be blotted out, so that times of refreshing may come from the presence of the Lord."
—Acts 3:19 (NKJV)

Devotional

There's a reason your phone has a reset button. When the software glitches or something breaks down, you don't throw the phone away—you reset it.

Repentance is God's reset button for the soul. It's not a punishment; it's a privilege. It's not a prison; it's a pathway. Through repentance, we don't just receive forgiveness—we gain restoration.

Peter's sermon in Acts 3 offers more than just cleansing of sin. It promises "times of refreshing" that follow genuine repentance. But the refreshing only comes after the repentance. The enemy will tell you repentance is painful and shameful. The truth? Repentance is liberating.

It's how you get unstuck. It's how you recover clarity. It's how you return to God's presence. You don't have to stay broken, distracted, or numb. Repent, and watch as God brings the refreshing wind of His Spirit to your weary soul.

Prayer

Father, thank You for Your goodness towards me. Thank You for being awesome in Your doing toward the sons of man. I declare there is no one like You in all the heavens and the earth. Thank you that Your tender mercies are renewed daily. Oh Yahweh, I desperately need You. I am a sinful person and I am guilty of breaking Your holy laws. Lord please help me! My human heart is deceitful above all things, and desperately wicked. Lord I need You! Thank You for hearing my petitions today. I love You and thank You in the wonderful name of Jesus! Amen.

Reflection Questions

What specific areas of your life do you need to bring before God in repentance today?

_____

_____

How have you viewed repentance in the past—burden or blessing?

_____

_____

What "times of refreshing" are you believing for after your repentance?

_____

_____

When God's Fire Falls

Scripture:

"Then the fire of the Lord fell and consumed the burnt sacrifice, and the wood and the stones and the dust, and it licked up the water that was in the trench." —**1 Kings 18:38 (NKJV)**

Devotional

Mount Carmel wasn't just a showdown between Elijah and the prophets of Baal—it was a revelation of what moves God. Elijah rebuilt the altar, laid the offering in place, and then prayed a prayer rooted not in showmanship, but in surrendered obedience.

Then it happened.

The fire of the Lord fell.

It was heaven's endorsement of a heart and altar properly prepared. The fire didn't fall when the people shouted. It didn't fall when they danced. It didn't even fall when Elijah rebuilt the altar. It fell when everything was in alignment and the sacrifice was laid bare.

God's fire always falls on sacrifice.

We want fire with no cost. We want power without surrender. But the fire of the Lord is drawn to holy places, broken altars, and laid-down lives. You can't microwave revival. You build the altar, you prepare the sacrifice, and then you call on God. And He answers.

Prayer

Father, thank You for Your lovingkindness and mercy towards me. There is nobody like You! Oh God, You are surely the God of Israel who made all creation in six days and rested on the seventh. You are great and awesome and who can thwart Your will? I lay my life down before You on Your altar. Please forgive me for all the times that I have taken myself off of the altar in the past. Please forgive me for all the times I have offered my life to you and then changed my mind. I offer myself to You now as a living sacrifice for Your exclusive use for life. I denounce the world and all that is in it. Please come and make me Yours for all time. Thank You for doing this for Your name sake and because You allow me to ask You for such a wonderful thing. I love You Father! Thank You in Jesus' name. Amen.

Reflection Questions

What areas of your life still need to be laid on the altar?

_____

_____

Are you seeking God's fire without offering a sacrifice?

_____

_____

What would it look like for you to fully surrender to the Lord today?

_____

_____

The Hidden Power of Fasting

Scripture:

"Is this not the fast that I have chosen: to loose the bonds of wickedness, to undo the heavy burdens, to let the oppressed go free, and that you break every yoke?" —**Isaiah 58:6 (NKJV)**

Devotional

Fasting is more than abstaining from food—it's an act of war in the spiritual realm. When done God's way, fasting breaks chains, undoes burdens, and sets the captives free. It's heaven's tool for heavenly outcomes.

But let's be honest—fasting is hard. That's because it crucifies the flesh. It brings to the surface the things you've used to numb yourself: food, media, entertainment, noise. When those things are stripped away, what's left is your raw heart before God.

And that's exactly the point.

God doesn't want religious duty; He desires a surrendered heart. In Isaiah 58, God rebukes those who fast outwardly but remain inwardly rebellious. He says the fast He's chosen involves compassion, justice, humility, and personal holiness.

Fasting is about alignment. It is a spiritual realignment of the body, soul, and spirit to heaven's frequency. And when you fast with the right heart, God moves mountains.

Prayer

Father, You hold all power in Your hands. No one can thwart You and none can defeat You. You faithfully delivered Israel from the hands of Pharoah and brought them out of the land of Egypt. No one can deliver and save like the Lord our God! Oh Lord... I offer myself to You today as a living sacrifice. Will You please help me to fast and pray through the help of the Holy Spirit? God, when I fast in my own strength I'm just a hungry Christian. I need Your power! Help me to deny myself for Your glory. Help me to fast in such a manner that You may be pleased, that You'll show me mercy and grant my petitions. Father, thank You for doing this that You may be glorified in my life. I love You and I ask this in Jesus' name. Amen.

Reflection Questions

Why are you fasting—or why have you been hesitant to?

_____

_____

In what ways has God used fasting to expose hidden things in your life?

_____

_____

What breakthroughs are you believing God for through your next fast?

_____

_____

DAY 14

Guarding the Gateways

Scripture:

"I will set nothing wicked before my eyes; I hate the work of those who fall away; it shall not cling to me." —**Psalm 101:3 (NKJV)**

Devotional

Your eyes, ears, and mind are the gateways to your soul. What you allow in will eventually manifest in your thoughts, desires, and behaviors. In a world saturated with ungodly media, seductive messaging, and moral confusion, guarding your gateways is not optional—it's essential.

David, a man after God's heart, made a personal vow: *"I will set nothing wicked before my eyes."* He understood the power of exposure. What you behold, you begin to desire. What you meditate on, you begin to replicate.

If Satan can infiltrate your life through what you watch, listen to, scroll through, or entertain, he will wage war against your sanctification. This is why pornography, gossip, violent media, ungodly music, and even certain relationships can quietly erode your spiritual strength. They're gateways.

But the opposite is also true. When you feed your soul with the Word of God, worship, truth-filled content, and righteous community, your spirit becomes sharp, alert, and full of light.

Prayer

Father, You are merciful and kind to the weak. You are a merciful God who loves the widow and the orphan. A holy God who sees all that men do in secret. Oh God, I have sinned before You and You alone by the things I have allowed to enter my eyes, ears and heart. Please forgive me for meditating on wicked things. Please forgive me for the vile things I have allowed my eyes, ears, and heart to consume. Please forgive me for compromising so that I could enjoy the pleasures of this world. Please help me that the words of my mouth, and the meditation of my heart, may be acceptable in Your sight, O Lord, my strength, and my redeemer. I need You so much Father and can't do this on my own. May You have mercy on my soul and grant my petitions. Thank you Father! In Jesus' name.

Reflection Questions

What types of media or entertainment have you allowed into your life that need to be removed?

_____

_____

Are your spiritual senses sharpened or dulled by what you regularly consume?

_____

_____

What boundaries will you set today to guard your spiritual gateways?

_____

_____

DAY 15

The Power of the Tongue

Scripture:

"Death and life are in the power of the tongue, and those who love it will eat its fruit." —**Proverbs 18:21 (NKJV)**

Devotional

Your words carry weight. They are not mere vibrations in the air; they are spiritual forces that either build or destroy, heal or wound, bless or curse. Scripture makes it plain: life and death are in your mouth.

God created the world through spoken word—and as His image-bearers, our words also shape environments, relationships, and outcomes. Jesus taught that we will give an account for every idle word (Matthew 12:36), reminding us that our speech has eternal significance.

Many believers sabotage their walk with God through negative self-talk, murmuring, gossip, and unholy declarations. Saying "I'll never change," "I always mess up," or "God isn't listening to me" reinforces spiritual defeat. But the tongue surrendered to Christ becomes a fountain of life—speaking truth, encouragement, correction, and worship.

Let your mouth become an instrument of righteousness. Speak the promises of God over your life. Declare what He says, not what fear or flesh says. When your tongue comes under submission to the Holy Spirit, so does the rest of your body.

Prayer

Father, thank You for being the God of all Creation. Power belongs to You. Thy kingdom come. Thy will be done. Father, I have been reckless with my tongue and the power of death and life contained in it. I have not been intentional in purposing my words. Please forgive me for all the ways I have spoken death over my calling, my giftings, myself and others in my life. Lord I repent right now before You. I offer my mouth and my breath to You that You may do with it as You will. Please always help me to be mindful of the power that You have given me and teach me how to use it properly. Thank You so much! In Jesus' name. Amen.

Reflection Questions

What patterns of speech do you need to repent of?

_____

_____

Are your words feeding faith or fueling fear?

_____

_____

How can you intentionally use your words today to speak life into someone else?

_____

_____

DAY 16

Sifted for Glory

Scripture:

"And the Lord said, 'Simon, Simon! Indeed, Satan has asked for you, that he may sift you as wheat. But I have prayed for you, that your faith should not fail; and when you have returned to Me, strengthen your brethren.'" —**Luke 22:31–32 (NKJV)**

Devotional

Trials don't always come because you've done something wrong. Sometimes, they come because you're about to do something right. Jesus knew Peter would fall—but He also knew Peter would rise. The enemy's goal was to destroy Peter through shame and failure. But Jesus had a better plan: redemption, restoration, and purpose.

To "sift" is to shake violently, to test and separate. Satan wanted to shake Peter so that his faith would fall apart. But Jesus didn't stop the sifting— He interceded through it. That's often how God works. He doesn't always remove the storm, but He strengthens you to endure it, and then uses the experience to refine you.

The same Peter who denied Christ became the bold apostle who preached at Pentecost. Why? Because the sifting stripped away his pride and self-reliance. It revealed his need for Jesus in a way that head knowledge never could.

So if you're being shaken, take heart. You're not being destroyed—you're being refined. The fire is not your end. It's your purification.

Prayer

Father, thank You for being the only wise God. Thank You for always having my absolute best in mind. I declare that no one loves me like You do and that You know best. Father, I have been guilty of doubting Your intentions for me at times in the past. Please forgive me for not believing You are exactly who You say You are and that You love me the way You say You do. Please help me to be still and know You are God when I go through the storms and trials of life. I love You! Thank You in Jesus' name. Amen.

Reflection Questions

Are you currently experiencing a "sifting" season? How are you responding?

_____

_____

What areas of your life is God refining through pressure or failure?

_____

_____

How can your story bring strength and hope to someone else?

_____

_____

DAY 17

The Voice of the Lord

Scripture:

"The voice of the Lord is powerful; the voice of the Lord is full of majesty. The voice of the Lord breaks the cedars, yes, the Lord splinters the cedars of Lebanon." —**Psalm 29:4–5 (NKJV)**

Devotional

God's voice isn't casual background noise. It is majestic, mighty, and capable of shaking the very foundations of creation. In Psalm 29, David paints a picture of the Lord's voice as something more forceful than any storm, more authoritative than any ruler, and more enduring than any obstacle.

The cedars of Lebanon were symbols of strength and stability in ancient Israel. Yet when the Lord speaks, even those mighty trees are splintered. That's the power of divine speech—able to break strongholds, disrupt systems, and shake what seemed unshakable.

His voice brings order out of chaos, life out of dust, and peace out of storms. This same voice that thundered over the waters in Genesis 1 now whispers to you through His Word and the Holy Spirit. Are you listening?

When God speaks, we must respond. His voice might bring conviction, but it also brings healing. It might disrupt, but only to rebuild. It might break, but only to bless.

Prayer

Thank You Father for being the Lord God Almighty who spoke forth the heavens and the earth! Thank You for having all power, grace, and sufficiency. Father, I confess that sometimes I do not heed Your voice when it comes to me. Please forgive me for all the times I did this. Please forgive me for the times when I have grieved Your Spirit by going my own way and trusting in my own understanding. Father, please help me to quiet down my spirit, to be still and know You are the Lord. Lord, You said Your sheep hear Your voice, and You know them, and they follow You. May You please grant me ears to hear what thus sayeth the Lord that I may follow You all the days of my life. Thank You Father. In Jesus' name. Amen.

Reflection Questions

How has the voice of the Lord disrupted your plans for a greater purpose?

_____

_____

Are there "cedars" in your life—false strengths—that God is trying to break?

_____

_____

What is one way you can quiet your life to better hear God today?

_____

_____

DAY 18

When God Hides You

Scripture:

"You are my hiding place; You shall preserve me from trouble; You shall surround me with songs of deliverance. Selah."
—Psalm 32:7 (NKJV)

Devotional

There are moments when God doesn't propel you into visibility—He hides you. While the world pushes platforms and popularity, God is often working in the secret place, shielding and shaping His servants for a time that is not yet.

Being hidden is not punishment; it's protection. It's preparation. Before David ever fought Goliath, he was hidden in the fields tending sheep. Before Moses delivered Israel, he spent forty years in the wilderness. Before Jesus began His public ministry, He lived thirty hidden years in Nazareth.

God hides us to heal us. He hides us to train us. He hides us to remove dependencies on human applause so we will walk only in His approval.

If you find yourself in a hidden season, rejoice. You are in the holy forge of God's process. He sees you. He surrounds you with songs of deliverance. And when the time is right, He will bring you forth like gold.

Prayer

Father, thank You for being Sovereign God of all creation. Thank You that nothing happens upon the face of the earth without Your knowledge of it. Father, please forgive me for the times I allowed myself to fret, doubt, and fear when things didn't go as I expected them to go. Thank You for Your perfect timing. Please help me with my unbelief and to trust that You are Sovereign and know what's best for me at all times. Thank You in Jesus' name. Amen.

Reflection Questions

Have you mistaken hiddenness for abandonment? What truth does today's Scripture reveal?

_____

_____

In what areas is God preserving you by keeping you out of the spotlight?

_____

_____

What might God be preparing you for during this season?

_____

_____

The Power of the Name

Scripture:

"Therefore God also has highly exalted Him and given Him the name which is above every name, that at the name of Jesus every knee should bow, of those in heaven, and of those on earth, and of those under the earth." —**Philippians 2:9–10 (NKJV)**

Devotional

There is power in the name of Jesus—immeasurable, unshakable, and eternal. This isn't poetic symbolism. It's divine authority. His name is above cancer, above addiction, above depression, above witchcraft, above poverty, above political kingdoms, and above demonic strongholds.

When you speak His name in faith, hell trembles. Chains loosen. Darkness flees. Hearts are mended. Bodies are healed. The heavens recognize the name. The earth must respond. And the demons have no choice but to bow in submission to it.

But the power of His name is only fully realized in the mouth of one who lives under His Lordship. You cannot declare "Jesus is Lord" while bowing to idols, compromise, or your own will. The name is not a magical formula. It is a representation of His presence, His person, and His power.

When we abide in Him, His name becomes our strong tower. And we who run to it are safe.

Prayer

Father, thank You that Your word is law. By Your word the heavens and the earth were created of old. Father, I have sinned by using the name of the Lord in vain. I have doubted in my heart that I am authorized to use Your great name in my life. Please forgive me for doubting You and Your holy word. Please help me with my unbelief and help me to speak boldly in Your name as I ought. Thank You. I ask in Jesus' name. Amen.

Reflection Questions

What situations in your life do you need to place under the authority of Jesus' name?

_____

_____

Have you used His name as a phrase or as a position of faith?

_____

_____

How can you live more intentionally under His Lordship?

_____

_____

DAY 20

The Remnant Rises

Scripture:

"Even so then, at this present time there is a remnant according to the election of grace." —**Romans 11:5 (NKJV)**

Devotional

In every generation, God reserves for Himself a remnant—a faithful few who have not bowed the knee to Baal, who refuse to compromise truth for convenience, and who walk in righteousness though the world mocks them.

The remnant is not popular.
The remnant is not trendy.
The remnant is not always visible.
But the remnant is powerful, preserved, and positioned for such a time as this.

We live in an age of great delusion, where lukewarm faith is celebrated and obedience to God is mocked as radicalism. But while many fall away, the remnant rises—not by might, nor by power, but by His Spirit.

These are the ones who will rebuild the ancient ruins. They will cry out for holiness and truth. They will not flinch in the face of persecution, nor be silenced by culture. They live not for applause, but for the pleasure of the King.

And if you're reading this with a burning in your heart, perhaps you are part of that remnant.

Prayer

Father, You are merciful and kind above all others. Thank You for always showing me Your great and unfailing love. Father, I have been lukewarm in many areas of my life. I have not sought You with my whole heart to resist compromise. I have not walked in holiness before You. Please forgive me. Lord please help me to not fall away, help me to walk uprightly before You always. Please help me to walk in holiness that I may be part of that faithful remnant. I love You! Thank You in Jesus' name! Amen.

Reflection Questions

What compromises have you been tempted to make in your walk with God?

_____

_____

Are you willing to stand alone if necessary in order to obey the Lord?

_____

_____

How can you remain faithful in an unfaithful generation?

_____

_____

DAY 21

Called Out of Babylon

Scripture:

"And I heard another voice from heaven, saying, 'Come out of her, my people, lest you share in her sins, and lest you receive of her plagues.'"
—Revelation 18:4 (NKJV)

Devotional

Babylon is more than a place—it is a spirit.
It is the seductive system of the world that entices the flesh, inflates pride, and mocks the holiness of God.
It preaches prosperity without purity.
It offers religion without repentance.
It sings of love but knows nothing of the cross.

And yet, in the midst of Babylon, God still has a people. A remnant.
And to them, He issues a clarion call:
"Come out of her, My people."

This call is not just about leaving a location—it's about a spiritual separation. It means cutting ties with ungodly alliances, compromising entertainment, unrepentant relationships, and worldly systems that dull our discernment and weaken our witness.

Like Lot fleeing Sodom, we are not to look back.
Like the Israelites leaving Egypt, we are not to long for the garlic and leeks of bondage.

If you belong to God, you can't live in Babylon and not be affected. So the Lord, in His mercy, says:

"Come out. Don't share in her sin. Don't suffer in her judgment."

Prayer

Father, Your name is holy. Thank You for Your holy ways. Thank You for Your lovingkindness towards me. Oh God, I have loved this world. I have loved my sin so that I did not want to come into the light with it. Please forgive me. May You have mercy on me. Please remove my heart of stone. Please give me a heart of flesh. Please give me Your holy desires that I may follow You and live. Thank You for this. I love You. Thank You in Jesus' name. Amen.

Reflection Questions

What "Babylonian" influences still have a place in your life?

_____

_____

Are there relationships, habits, or entertainments God is calling you to walk away from?

_____

_____

How will you respond to God's command to "come out"?

_____

_____

DAY 22

You Were Bought With a Price

Scripture:

"For you were bought at a price; therefore glorify God in your body and in your spirit, which are God's." —**1 Corinthians 6:20 (NKJV)**

Devotional

The cross was not cheap.
It wasn't painless.
It wasn't a generic, symbolic gesture.
It was costly.

You were bought with the price of blood—holy, undefiled, sacrificial blood. The Son of God gave His life to redeem you from the penalty and power of sin. You don't belong to yourself anymore. You're not your own master. You are His.

This truth should radically transform how we live.

We are not free to use our bodies however we please, entertain our minds with whatever we desire, or justify our actions by what feels good. We are called to glorify God—not just with our words, but with our bodies, our spirits, our choices, and our very existence.

When you recognize the price that was paid, you won't live casually. You'll live consecrated.

158

Prayer

Father, thank You for sending Your Son Jesus to die for me. Thank You for loving me so much that You would send Your only begotten Son to take my place on the cross. Father, there are so many ways that I haven't glorified You in my body and spirit. Please forgive me. Please help me to do this by the power and help of the Holy Spirit. Thank You for Your great love Father! Thank You in Jesus' name. Amen.

Reflection Questions

Do you live like you belong to God or like you still belong to yourself?

_____

_____

In what areas of your life have you not fully surrendered to God's ownership?

_____

_____

How can you glorify God with your body and spirit today?

_____

_____

Godly Sorrow That Leads to Repentance

Scripture:

> *"For godly sorrow produces repentance leading to salvation, not to be regretted; but the sorrow of the world produces death."*
> —**2 Corinthians 7:10 (NKJV)**

Devotional

Not all sorrow is created equal.
Worldly sorrow says, "I'm sorry I got caught."
Godly sorrow says, "I'm grieved because I've sinned against a holy God."

One leads to a temporary change.
The other leads to transformation.

Godly sorrow is a deep work of the Spirit—it's not manufactured by emotions alone. It is birthed when the veil is pulled back and we see our sin through God's eyes. It produces more than tears. It produces a turning—a break from sin and a longing for righteousness.

This is what happened to David when he cried, *"Against You, and You only, have I sinned"* (Psalm 51:4). This is what happened in the hearts of those who heard Peter's sermon at Pentecost and were "cut to the heart" (Acts 2:37).

You can't conjure up godly sorrow, but you can ask God for it.

And when you do, He will meet you at the altar, tear open the hidden places of your heart, and plant in you a grief—not unto shame, but unto salvation.

Prayer

Father, thank You for Your compassionate heart. Thank You for loving me always and with an unfailing love. Father, I have sinned by breaking Your laws in many ways. Please forgive me for sinning against You. I've tried but I just can't do it in my own strength and power. Please create in me a clean heart and renew within me a right spirit. Please convict me that I might gain Your godly sorrow that will lead me to repentance in Your sight. I need Your help so badly. I can't do it on my own. Father, if You don't help me then I won't be helped. Thank You for being so merciful to me and always coming to my rescue. I ask these things in Jesus' name. Amen.

Reflection Questions

Have you experienced godly sorrow or just worldly regret?

_____

_____

What sin in your life do you tend to justify or downplay?

_____

_____

What would it look like for you to truly repent and turn?

_____

_____

DAY 24

Return to Your First Love

Scripture:

"Nevertheless I have this against you, that you have left your first love. Remember therefore from where you have fallen; repent and do the first works, or else I will come to you quickly and remove your lampstand from its place-unless you repent." —**Revelation 2:4–5 (NKJV)**

Devotional

The Ephesian church had many admirable qualities—zeal, doctrinal soundness, hard work. But Jesus still issued a rebuke: *"You have left your first love."*

It wasn't that they stopped believing.
It wasn't that they quit doing good.
It was that their **love** had grown cold.

This is a warning to us all. You can attend church, serve in ministry, defend truth—and still have a heart that's drifted from intimacy with God. Busyness is not the same as closeness. Activity is not the same as affection.

Jesus calls us to remember where we once stood in passionate devotion. To repent from our spiritual apathy. And to return to those early acts of love—those mornings of seeking His face, those hours spent in worship with no agenda, those times we opened His Word just to know Him more.

First love is not about emotional highs.

It's about prioritizing Him.

It's about loving Him with all your heart, soul, mind, and strength (Mark 12:30).

Prayer

Father, thank You for Your faithfulness. Thank You that You have only been good to me throughout the course of my life. Yet I have turned my back to You in many ways. I have loved the world and the things of the world. Please forgive me for hurting Your heart and for not loving my First Love. Please give me a new heart that will seek You in all ways and at all times. Please lead me back to You with Your goodness. Thank You so much. In Jesus' name. Amen.

Reflection Questions

Has your relationship with God grown cold or routine?

_____

_____

What "first works" do you need to return to?

_____

_____

What steps will you take today to rekindle intimacy with the Lord?

_____

_____

Wholly Set Apart

Scripture:

> *"But you are a chosen generation, a royal priesthood, a holy nation,*
> *His own special people, that you may proclaim the praises of Him who*
> *called you out of darkness into His marvelous light."*
> **—1 Peter 2:9 (NKJV)**

Devotional

God has not merely called you to believe—He has called you to belong. You are not common. You are not ordinary. You are set apart.

You are His priest. His ambassador. His own special possession. But with that identity comes a holy charge: to live differently than the world.

Holiness isn't legalism—it's loyalty.
It's not perfection—it's separation.
To be holy is to say, "Lord, I will go where You go, speak what You speak, and avoid what grieves You."

In a world that blurs every moral line, your life is meant to draw the line in Christ. You're not just called out of darkness—you're called into marvelous light. The difference should be visible. Tangible. Evident.

This means purity in your relationships, integrity in your work, and reverence in your worship. You weren't saved to blend in. You were saved to stand out—for His glory.

Prayer

Father, thank You for choosing me before the beginning of the world. Thank You that You have chosen me to be Yours. Please forgive me for the ways in which I have adopted the world's ways in my life. Please forgive me for loving the world and the things of this world more than I have loved You. I repent right now in the name of Jesus! Please help me Father by Your Spirit. I ask these things in Jesus' name. Amen.

Reflection Questions

In what areas of your life do you need to be more set apart?

_____

_____

Are there habits, relationships, or mindsets keeping you tied to the world?

_____

_____

What would it look like to fully embrace your identity as God's royal priesthood?

_____

_____

DAY 26

The Narrow Road

Scripture:

"Enter by the narrow gate; for wide is the gate and broad is the way that leads to destruction, and there are many who go in by it. Because narrow is the gate and difficult is the way which leads to life, and there are few who find it." **—Matthew 7:13–14 (NKJV)**

Devotional

Jesus didn't sugarcoat it. He said the path to life is narrow—and difficult—and few will find it.

That means following Him isn't about convenience. It's about conviction.

The narrow road demands sacrifice. It asks you to deny your flesh, endure trials, reject cultural trends, and walk in obedience—especially when it costs you.

The broad road feels safer. It's filled with people, entertainment, applause, and self-indulgence. But that road leads to destruction. The crowd is big because the standard is low.

But the narrow path—though costly—is glorious. It leads to eternal life. Every stumble becomes strength. Every sacrifice becomes worship. Every tear sown in obedience reaps a harvest of righteousness.

Jesus walked the narrow road before you. He endured the shame, the rejection, and the cross so that you could follow Him into glory. He's not calling you anywhere He hasn't gone first.

166

So take courage. Stay the course. The road may be narrow—but it leads to the presence of God.

Prayer

Father, thank You that You are holy and good. Thank You that Your ways are higher than mine. Father, you have given me everything through Your Son Jesus, yet I have compromised and traded in Your promises for the golden calves of this present world. Please forgive me. Please help me to live circumspectly before You. Please do this through me by Your Holy Spirit. I offer myself to you as a holy sacrifice. In Jesus' name. Amen.

Reflection Questions

Have you ever found yourself drifting toward the broad road of comfort or compromise?

_____

_____

What daily choices are required to stay on the narrow path?

_____

_____

Who is walking the narrow road with you—and who needs to be encouraged to get on it?

_____

_____

Burn the Ships! Burn the Charts!

Scripture:

"So Elisha left him and went back. He took his yoke of oxen and slaughtered them. He burned the plowing equipment to cook the meat and gave it to the people, and they ate. Then he set out to follow Elijah and became his servant. —**1 Kings 19:21 (NIV)**

Devotional

When Elijah called Elisha to follow him, Elisha didn't hedge his bets.

He didn't say, "Let me keep one ox just in case this prophet thing doesn't work out."
He burned the plow and butchered the oxen. He made a public, irreversible declaration:
"I'm not going back."

There comes a moment in every believer's life when God says,
"It's time to burn the ships and burn the charts."
No more clinging to the past. No more safety nets. No more backup plans that give you room to disobey and return to the land from whence you came.

Jesus said no one who puts his hand to the plow and looks back is fit for the kingdom of God (Luke 9:62). If you're going to follow Him, it must be forward only.

Maybe for you, the "plow" is a toxic relationship. A compromising career. A sinful comfort. Or simply the fear of stepping out in faith. Whatever it is—if it's holding you back—it's time to burn it.

Not out of recklessness, but out of reverence. Because when you give God your all, He gives you more than you imagined.

Prayer

Father, thank you for being so kind to me and giving me Your unfailing love. Will you please show me what I've been holding onto? Give me the courage to burn the plow and follow You completely. I never want to go back ever again in my life. Please help me to move forward—closer to You, closer to Your will, and deeper into Your presence. Thank you in Jesus' name. Amen.

Reflection Questions

What are the "ships" or "plows" you need to burn in your walk with God?

_____

_____

Are there safety nets or compromises you've been reluctant to let go of?

_____

_____

What might God be waiting to release once you fully commit?

_____

_____

The Oil Is in the Obedience

Scripture:

> *"Elisha said, 'Go around and ask all your neighbors for empty jars. Don't ask for just a few.' ... She left him and shut the door behind her and her sons. They brought the jars to her and she kept pouring."*
> **—2 Kings 4:3–5 (NIV)**

Devotional

When the widow cried out for help, Elisha gave her an instruction that didn't make logical sense:
Collect empty jars. As many as you can.

He didn't say, "Go find oil." He didn't say, "Borrow money." He said, "Collect emptiness."
It was in her obedience to that word—not the oil itself—that the miracle was released.

She obeyed, shut the door behind her, and began pouring. And the oil did not stop flowing until there were no more vessels left.

This is a picture of spiritual obedience. The miraculous provision of God is released through simple acts of faith. If she had argued or hesitated—if she had gathered only a few jars—the flow of oil would have ended sooner.

You may be praying for an overflow, but are you making room? You may be asking God to fill you, but have you brought Him your empty jars?

Obedience creates capacity.
The oil of God's anointing will never run out when there is a vessel ready to receive it.

Prayer

Father, thank You for supplying all of my needs according to Your riches in glory by Christ Jesus. Please forgive me for the times I've been disobedient to the leading of the Holy Spirit when You were attempting to supply my need. I love You. Thank You in Jesus' name. Amen.

Reflection Questions

What step of obedience has God been prompting you to take?

_____

_____

Are there areas where you're waiting for oil but haven't yet gathered the jars?

_____

_____

What would it look like for you to "shut the door" and trust God privately in faith?

_____

_____

DAY 29

A New Identity

Scripture:

"Therefore, if anyone is in Christ, he is a new creation; old things have passed away; behold, all things have become new."
—2 Corinthians 5:17 (NKJV)

Devotional

The moment you surrendered to Christ, your identity was rewritten in heaven.
No longer are you defined by your past mistakes, your family history, or the labels the world gave you. **You are a new creation.**

But many believers still walk around in the tattered clothes of their old identity—ashamed, insecure, afraid. They've been born again but haven't embraced the fullness of their heavenly identity.

You are no longer a slave to sin.
You are no longer rejected, forgotten, or alone.
You are not who you were.

You are chosen.
You are beloved.
You are seated with Christ in heavenly places (Eph. 2:6).
You are a child of the King, clothed in righteousness and empowered by His Spirit.

But here's the key: You must walk in what God has declared over you. If you keep speaking defeat, doubt, and death over yourself, you will never live the abundant life Christ died to give you.

Tear off the grave clothes. Put on the robe of righteousness.
Stand in your God-given identity—because the enemy is terrified of the day you realize who you really are.

Prayer

Father, thank You for giving me a new identity in Christ. Thank You for making me Yours. Please forgive me for the times when I walk in doubt about who You say I am. Please help me with my unbelief and teach me how to walk in the freedom and power that the Holy Spirit provides for me. Thank You for loving me. In Jesus' name. Amen.

Reflection Questions

What false labels or identities are you still holding onto?

_____

_____

How can you practically begin living from your new identity in Christ?

_____

_____

Which Scripture truths can you begin declaring daily to reinforce your God-given identity?

_____

_____

Repairers of the Breach

Scripture:

> *"Those from among you shall build the old waste places;*
> *You shall raise up the foundations of many generations;*
> *And you shall be called the Repairer of the Breach,*
> *The Restorer of Streets to Dwell In."*
> **—Isaiah 58:12 (NKJV)**

Devotional

You were not saved to sit on the sidelines.
You were saved to rebuild what hell tried to destroy.

This is the call for every believer in this hour:
Rebuild the broken altars. Restore the ancient paths. Repair the breach.

There's a breach in the wall of the Church today—a gaping hole where truth has leaked out and compromise has rushed in.
God is looking for people who will stand in the gap, not with opinions or popularity, but with fire, faith, and faithfulness.

He is raising up a remnant—unashamed of the gospel, unafraid of man, and unwilling to water down the Word.
These are the ones who cry out for holiness, who weep between the porch and the altar, who tremble at His Word.

And here's the astonishing part:
You are one of them.

It's no accident that you're reading this book and that you've made it to this point.
God has been rebuilding you so He can rebuild through you.

You've been set apart to carry His glory, to reestablish His standard, and to revive your generation.

You are a Repairer of the Breach.

Now, onward Christian Soldier. Go and take dominion for the Lord and the Kingdom of Heaven!!

Prayer

Father, thine is the kingdom and the glory and the power forever. Thank You for choosing me to do this good work for You. Please forgive me for the times I walked in unbelief. Please help me to walk in holy boldness that I may be obedient to Your will. May You be with me like You were with Moses and Joshua. Please use me for Your glory as You see fit. I love You. Thank You in Jesus' name. Amen.

Reflection Questions

What areas of your home, community, or church are in spiritual ruin and need rebuilding?

_____

_____

How has God been preparing you to stand in the gap?

_____

_____

What legacy do you want to leave for the next generation?

_____

_____

Scripture Index
(Organized by Chapter)

Introduction

- Hebrews 12:14–17
- Proverbs 14:34
- Jeremiah 2:13
- 2 Timothy 3:5

Chapter 1 – The Idol of American Christianity

- Acts 19:13–16

Chapter 2 – A Fiend in Sheep's Clothing

- Matthew 7:22–23
- Revelation 2:6
- Revelation 2:15
- Acts 6:5
- 2 Tim. 3:5
- Luke 8:4–15
- 2 Timothy 4:3–4
- 1 John 3:8
- Luke 18:18–25
- Matthew 7:16

Chapter 3 – Blended Threads and Broken Altars

- Leviticus 20:26
- Exodus 23:23-24
- John 14:6
- 1 Timothy 4:1
- Exodus 20:25
- 1 Samuel 15:23
- Leviticus 19:31
- Revelation 18:4
- Acts 19:18-19
- Psalms 22:3
- Revelation 2:20
- Judges 16:18-21
- Ezekiel 8:6-12
- Revelation 12:9
- Revelation 20:2
- Psalms 62:11
- 1 Corinthian 12:11
- Deuteronomy 18:10-12
- 2 Kings 9:30-33
- 2 Kings 9:22
- 1 Kings 18:30
- Acts 2
- Malachi 1:6–10
- Genesis 12:7
- Genesis 13:4
- Genesis 15:9–10

Chapter 6 – Rebuilding the Altar

- Genesis 22:3
- Hebrews 11:19
- Genesis 22:5
- Psalm 139:23–24
- Joel 2:13
- James 4:8–10
- 1 Peter 4:18
- 1 Samuel 2:30
- 1 John 1:6–7
- 1 John 1:5
- John 3:20–21
- Isaiah 60:1
- Ephesians 5:14
- Hebrews 12:14
- John 8:31–32
- Leviticus 6:13
- John 6:35
- Ephesians 6:17
- Psalm 119:105
- Matthew 7:24–27

A Final Word

- Hebrews 1:7
- Romans 13:11
- 1 Kings 18:30-39

Rebuilding the Altar: 30 Days of Repentance, Renewal, and Fire

- 1 Peter 2:9
- Matthew 7:13–14
- 1 Kings 19:21
- 2 Kings 4:3–5
- 2 Corinthians 5:17
- Isaiah 58:12

References

Adams, John.
"The Constitution was made only for a moral and religious people. It is wholly inadequate to the government of any other." Letter to the Massachusetts Militia, October 11, 1798.

Arizona Christian University.
"Inaugural CRC Study: Dangerously Low Percentage of Americans Hold Biblical Worldview." Cultural Research Center at Arizona Christian University. March 24, 2020. https://www.arizonachristian. edu/2020/03/24/inaugural-crc-study-dangerously-low-percentage-of-americans-hold-biblical-worldview/

Baucham, Voddie.
"People don't reject the Bible because it contradicts itself. They reject it because it contradicts them." Quote attributed to Baucham in public sermons and writings.

Clement of Alexandria.
"Miscellanies (Stromata), Book II." Translated by William Wilson. In *The Ante-Nicene Fathers*, edited by Alexander Roberts and James Donaldson. Vol. 2. Peabody, MA: Hendrickson, 1994.

Eslit, Nila.
"Why Christians Should Not Celebrate Halloween." *Meer.com*, October 25, 2019. https://www.meer.com/en/58292-why-christians-should-not-celebrate-halloween#:~:text=Anton%20LaVey%2C%20the%20founder%20of,Welcome%20to%20Halloween.

Havner, Vance.
"We are not going to move this world by criticism of it nor conformity to it, but by the combustion within it of lives ignited by the Spirit of God." Quoted in *When God Breaks Through* by Vance Havner. Grand Rapids, MI: Baker Books, 1990.

Irenaeus.
Against Heresies, Book I, Chapter 26. Translated by Alexander Roberts and William Rambaut. In *The Ante-Nicene Fathers*, Vol. 1. Peabody, MA: Hendrickson, 1994.

Keener, Craig S.
IVP Bible Background Commentary: New Testament. Downers Grove, IL: IVP Academic, 1993.

Lester Sumrall

1. Sumrall, Lester. *Alien Entities: Are They Real?* South Bend, IN: Whitaker House, 1995.

2. Sumrall, Lester. *Demons: The Answer Book.* Tulsa, OK: Harrison House, 1981.

MacArthur, John.
"When church becomes entertainment, and the pulpit becomes a platform for opinion rather than exposition, we are no longer shepherds—we are performers. And the sheep are starving." Quote attributed in multiple sermons and articles; MacArthur, John. *Ashamed of the Gospel: When the Church Becomes Like the World.* Wheaton, IL: Crossway Books, 1993.

Meer.com (Eslit, Nila).
See Eslit, Nila. "Why Christians Should Not Celebrate Halloween."

Northwestern Mutual.
"Nearly 70% of Americans Say Financial Uncertainty Has Made Them Feel Depressed and Anxious, According to Northwestern Mutual 2025 Planning & Progress Study." *Northwestern Mutual Newsroom.* June 3,

2025. https://news.northwesternmutual.com/2025-06-03-Nearly-70-of-Americans-Say-Financial-Uncertainty-Has-Made-Them-Feel-Depressed-and-Anxious

"Financial uncertainty is having a profound emotional impact." *2025 Planning and Progress Study.* Accessed July 2025. https://news.northwesternmutual.com/planning-and-progress-study-2025

ProgramBusiness.com.
"Widespread Financial Anxiety in the U.S. Hits New Highs, Especially Among Younger Generations." ProgramBusiness News, 2025. https://programbusiness.com/news/widespread-financial-anxiety-in-the-u-s-hits-new-highs-especially-among-younger-generations

Ravenhill, Leonard.
Why Revival Tarries. Minneapolis, MN: Bethany House Publishers, 1959.
Quotes include:

- "The church used to be a lightning bolt—now it's a cruise ship."

- "We don't need another method. We need another Pentecost."

- "There are many in our churches who are not backslidden—they've never front-slid."

Rebecca Brown, MD

1. Brown, Rebecca. *He Came to Set the Captives Free.* New Kensington, PA: Whitaker House, 1992.

2. Brown, Rebecca. *Prepare for War.* New Kensington, PA: Whitaker House, 1992.

Spurgeon, Charles H.
Anecdotes and Illustrations. Grand Rapids, MI: Baker Book House, 1979.
"A religion that never suffices to govern a man's behavior will never save his soul."

Stanley, Charles.
"The fear of the Lord is the beginning of obedience. Without it, we reduce God to a God of our own making—one who is expected to tolerate everything and judge nothing." Quoted from *In Touch Ministries* broadcast archives, accessed July 2025.

Washington, George.
Farewell Address, September 19, 1796. Quoted from *A Compilation of the Messages and Papers of the Presidents*, ed. James D. Richardson. Washington, D.C.: Government Printing Office, 1899.

Wilkerson, David.
The Vision. Old Tappan, NJ: Revell, 1973.
Quotes include:

- "Our churches are filled with people who've made decisions but have never made disciples."

- "If God removed His hand from America today, most churches wouldn't even know it for weeks."

- "In many churches today, the Holy Spirit could leave and no one would notice…"

YouTube (Nick Jones).
"A Pastor Has A Chilling Encounter With Jesus Himself, Who Delivers An Urgent Message!" YouTube video, 1:32:57. Posted May 24, 2023. https://youtu.be/3Z-DUgJicYY?si=6IWdSWbucV5Ss0RQ

Glossary of Terms

Altar of the Lord – A spiritual place of sacrifice, surrender, and communion with God. In the Old Testament, it was a physical structure used for offerings. For the believer today, it symbolizes the heart posture of yielding fully to God's will and repenting of sin.

Anointing – The empowerment of the Holy Spirit that enables a believer to function in their God-ordained purpose. It is not merely emotional or external but rooted in submission to God and holiness of life.

Apostasy – The act of falling away from or abandoning the faith, often by embracing false doctrines, compromising truth, or living in willful sin while claiming godliness.

Babylon (spiritual) – Symbolic of worldly systems, idolatry, compromise, and rebellion against God. In this book, it often refers to the spirit of confusion and corruption that infiltrates churches and believers.

Carnality – Living according to the desires of the flesh rather than by the Spirit of God. A carnal Christian prioritizes pleasure, comfort, and worldly pursuits over obedience and holiness.

Conviction – The internal awareness of sin prompted by the Holy Spirit. It is a gift from God that leads to repentance and transformation, not to be confused with condemnation.

Deliverance – The act of being set free from spiritual bondage, oppression, or demonic influence. True deliverance requires repentance, renunciation of sin, and the authority of Jesus Christ.

False gospel – A distorted or diluted version of the gospel that omits repentance, the lordship of Christ, or the call to holiness. It offers comfort without conviction and grace without truth.

Fiend in Sheep's Clothing – A person or spirit masquerading as godly while promoting deception, compromise, or false teaching, either knowingly or unknowingly. This phrase is a play on "wolf in sheep's clothing" and exposes spiritual imposters.

Fire of God – A symbol of God's purifying presence, judgment, and power. In Scripture, His fire consumes offerings and cleanses hearts. It represents God's response to genuine sacrifice and devotion.

Godly sorrow – Deep spiritual grief over sin that leads to true repentance. This only comes from God and unlike worldly sorrow, which brings regret or shame, godly sorrow produces transformation and restores relationship with God (2 Cor. 7:10).

Holiness – A life set apart for God, marked by purity, obedience, and reverence. Holiness is not perfection but the daily pursuit of becoming more like Christ through the Spirit's power.

Idolatry – Anything that takes the place of God in one's heart or life. This includes not only statues or false gods, but also people, ideologies, entertainment, possessions, and even religious practices when misaligned with God's truth.

Nicolaitans – A group rebuked in Revelation for their compromise with pagan practices and teachings. Symbolically, they represent modern-day Christians or churches who blend worldly culture with Christian faith.

Repentance – A complete turning away from sin and self toward God. It involves a change of heart, mind, and direction. Repentance is not just remorse—it is the beginning of spiritual transformation.

Rebuilding the Altar – The spiritual act of restoring one's intimate fellowship with the Lord through confession, repentance, worship, and surrender. It involves forsaking compromise and rededicating oneself to truth and holiness.

Remnant – A faithful few who remain true to God despite widespread apostasy or compromise. In Scripture, the remnant carries the burden of intercession and revival, often misunderstood or rejected by the majority.

Sanctification – The ongoing process of being made holy by the Spirit of God. It is both a positional reality in Christ and a daily walk in obedience, requiring surrender, faith, and perseverance.

Syncretism – The blending of different belief systems, especially mixing Christianity with worldly ideologies or pagan practices. Syncretism undermines biblical faith and fosters spiritual deception.

Worldliness – The adoption of values, behaviors, and priorities that oppose God's holy kingdom. Worldliness is not merely external actions, but a heart that prioritizes self, pleasure, or culture over God's truth.

About the Author

Michael M. Dillard is a passionate evangelist, preacher and teacher of righteousness, called to point the Body of Christ back to holiness, repentance, and unwavering obedience to Christ. A retired U.S. Navy Chief Petty Officer (Submarines), he brings the same discipline, integrity, and courage from his 22 years of faithful military service into his service for the Lord.

As an evangelist, preacher, and teacher, Michael speaks from a place of deep conviction and lived experience.

His writing is not theoretical—it's forged by the fire of the Holy Spirit. He is known for his fearless stance on biblical truth, especially in confronting the spirit of compromise within the modern Church.

The Lord has also anointed Michael to equip the saints in the areas of spiritual warfare and biblical manhood—calling the body of Christ to walk in their godly authority, take dominion on the earth, and live as overcomers through the power of the Holy Spirit.

He resides on the tropical island of Oahu in Hawaiʻi, with his beautiful wife Angela, where they serve together in ministry, missions, and outreach. When he's not writing, working out or watching sea turtles at Kahana Bay, you'll probably find him somewhere praising the Lord, hosting his faith-forward podcast *Fully Submitted with Brother Mike*, or passed out on the long couch with his Queen Angela the Beautiful and their funny little dog Mr. Bojangles.

Connect with Michael

If this book has challenged or encouraged you, I would love to hear from you!

Connect or collaborate with me through the following channels:

Email: fullysubmitted4christ@gmail.com

Social Media:
LinkedIn: linkedin.com/in/michaelmdillard

www.ingramcontent.com/pod-product-compliance
Lightning Source LLC
Chambersburg PA
CBHW050441150626
46551CB00028B/934